RIPPLES OF
HEAVEN

*Changing the World through Mentoring –
One Discipleship Relationship at a Time*

LORI ORANDER

Quantity sales special discounts are available on quantity purchases by corporations, associations, and others. For details, contact the publisher at the address above.

Orders by U.S. and Canada trade bookstores and wholesalers. Email info@ BeyondPublishing.net

The Beyond Publishing Speakers Bureau can bring authors to your live event. For more information or to book an event contact the Beyond Publishing Speakers Bureau speak@BeyondPublishing.net

The Author can be reached directly at BeyondPublishing.net

Manufactured and printed in the United States of America distributed globally by BeyondPublishing.net

BEYOND
PUBLISHING

New York | Los Angeles | London | Sydney

ISBN Hardcover: 978-1-637921-50-0

ISBN Softcover: 978-1-637921-51-7

DEDICATION

This book is dedicated to my parents, Tom and Nancy Childs, my forever mentors who modeled authentic, sacrificial relationships and taught me to love hard.

I also dedicate this book to Pastor Bob and Pat Jones, who opened their home and their hearts to a college girl and her friends so they could be discipled in the ways of Jesus.

ENDORSEMENTS

I have had the great privilege of knowing Lori Orander over the last six years in the context of regional ministry and now have had the awesome privilege of reading her recent book, Ripples of Heaven. When I first picked up the manuscript, it was the bi-line, "Changing the world through Mentoring --- One Discipleship Relationship at a Time", that really caught my attention because when I think of Lori and her impact on individuals, I think of the phrase "world changer". One of the many things I appreciate about Lori is that her stated values are her actual values. She's not someone in public that she isn't in private. She actually lives this stuff out in real time. Knowing this is true about the author makes me receive the tremendous equipping that this book has to offer. She has actually pioneered in the area of mentoring and discipleship, especially with the emerging generation, in such a way that I have personally seen firsthand the beautiful fruit from these relationships. How so? Because some of these names mentioned in the book are people I personally know and highly esteem; and as the adage goes, "fruit don't lie!"

One of the poignant features of Ripples of Heaven is the power of testimony and the vehicle of story that lets us peer into both Lori's mentoring process and outcome. From Lori's own story to many of those she has discipled shared in this work, the reader will be stirred to 'go into all the world and make disciples'. The book is striking in that it is both inspiring and practical, not just a theological treatise but a compelling "how to". Mentoring/coaching seems to have become somewhat of a buzz term in modern Christianity, but still remains vague and for many, an unfulfilled longing. Many 'sons and daughters' out there long for a connection with an older, wiser person who will help speak into their spiritual/personal formation and offer guidance, yet there aren't enough spiritual mothers and fathers who have the discipleship tools to make this both fruitful and enjoyable. This is honestly one of the best books I have read on moving this topic from theory to one that can be practiced with humble confidence. I personally am renewing my commitment to pour into this next generation by finding my next 'Timothy'. I thank Lori for both this book but even more so for the cost of laying down her life over countless hours to see Christ formed in hearts. I cannot recommend this book highly enough!

Marvin Adams
Senior Leader SparrowsHouseMinistries

"I heard Pastor Bill Johnson (Bethel Church) suggest once that we don't study to teach, but to learn, to ingest. Then,when it's time to teach, we break off a part of our lives and give it away. Jesus did this (literally). And, Lori has done it in the book you're holding. I've known Lori for 20 years. I've watched her worship Jesus, love and honor her husband, raise her children and pour out her life on behalf of others. And, I can testify that she's the real deal. This book is a piece of her life, not perfect, but honest, powerful and rippling. This is just a portion of her story. Her story can be your story. If you long to see the life of Jesus replicated in and through your life, take this book. Read it. Ingest it. Walk it out. And watch the fruit of your life and love in Christ feed others, affecting generations! "

S. Randall Gooder
Senior Pastor Indy Vineyard Church, Indianapolis

"Timely. Effective. Real. Lori's testimonies and accounts in Ripples of Heaven effortlessly capture the heart and soul behind the Titus 2 call for older men and women to teach and raise up the next generation. From the onset, she not only teaches the mentor how to 'plant the seeds' but also offers the perspective of the reaper- the student, who in many cases, has grown up and on to mentor young people of their own. The rule of multiplication is alive and well throughout Ripples of Heaven, and the reader will do well to take from the gold that is detailed and evidenced in both Lori's writing and her life."

Kelly A Williams
Author, Founder, Table Ministries

"Lori Orander delivers a timely encouragement to God's people. She shares practical insight from living a life of intentional discipleship over the last three decades. This book will significantly impact your life… if you let it!"

Josh Heaston
Director of Christian Mission,
YMCA of Greater Indianapolis

"Few people have the authority to speak on mentorship the way that Lori does. She really lives this message every single day. I know that so many lives – including my own – have already been impacted by the way Lori does discipleship. I can't wait for so many more to not only be inspired, but also be equipped to live out this kind of mentoring in their own lives through reading this book. Let Lori's stories and wisdom empower you to start being the disciple maker you already are!! The world is truly going to be changed through this book in action."

Bryson Satariano
Active Ministry Manager, Delight Ministries, Nashville, TN

"Ripples of Heaven" by Lori Orander is a must-read book for Christian believers in every stage of their walk with Jesus. Lori not only articulates with passion and purpose the Great Commission of making disciples through mentoring relationships, but she recounts her life demonstration of this. This book is more than a 'how-to manual'; it takes the call and process of discipleship to the heart level. The 'Going Deeper' sections at the end of each chapter provide powerful questions and reflection before the Lord to help spur your own personal growth. You will be inspired, challenged, equipped, and encouraged as you read how YOUR life has been created to leave a legacy of sons and daughters of God. If there is one thing we keep seeing repetitively that is a missing crucial ingredient in the modern church, it is discipleship. This book release is 'for such a time as this' and will help equip the body of Christ into all that Jesus has created it to be."

Jesse and Jessica Cupp
Senior Leaders of Overflow Church, Indianapolis

"When Laura and I read Ripples of Heaven, we were both inspired, challenged, and moved to mentor and disciple others who will, in turn, mentor and disciple others. Lori brings us great practical advice from decades of experience on not just the "why" of mentoring but the "how" to go about it. This is a complete mentoring and discipling guide which, in turn, mentors the reader on best practices. We hope to use this as a resource within the mentoring ministry of the church we serve. Thank you, Lori, for making a Kingdom impact through this book!"

Rick and Laura Grover
East 91st Street Christian Church
Indianapolis, IN

CONTENTS

ACKNOWLEDGMENTS

With deepest gratitude and a Momma's heart of love, I thank my two incredible sons and all the precious, spiritual daughters that I have had the privilege to walk alongside for the past 3 decades. May you continually fan your flames of love for Jesus and go after Him with all that is within you! Never forget to take someone with you as you go; and continually tell your stories to the next generation! I especially want to thank those who contributed to this book by sharing their own personal stories and testimonies of how disciples go on to make disciples who make disciples, like Ripples of Heaven: Natalie Showalter, Erin Barnes, Sarah Robinson, Nancy Hendrickson, Morgan Julian, Ashlie Cook, Tara Stiver, Lindsey Frazee, Bailey Orander, Monica Jones, Heather Jesse, Jasmine Orander, Luke & Sarah Robinson, Stephen & Becca Morris, and Connor & Julia Lukas.

And many thanks to Michael and the incredible team at Beyond Publishing!

FORWARD

This world needs spiritual fathers and mothers.

This world needs you.

It is an exciting time to be alive on the earth! I believe we are in the beginning stages of the third Great Awakening and possibly the greatest revival this world has ever seen! This means that millions of people throughout the world and in your own neighborhood are going to be **born** again into the Family of God. These new children of God are going to need mothers and fathers in the faith to help them grow up into mature sons and daughters of God! This is what Jesus called making disciples.

I believe the best way to make disciples is to invite them into mentoring relationships!

This world needs spiritual mentors. This world needs you.

There is no lack of information in the world.

There is a lack of loving relationships.

Recently on the news, in the wake of more mass shootings in our nation, I heard these statistics: The top three commonalities between these troubled shooters over the past 10 years are consistently listed as **isolation, loneliness, and a lack of support or connection.** 27% of Millennials say they have no close friends. 23% said they had no acquaintances at all.

We were not meant to do life alone; we were meant to do life together.

Though the word *mentoring* is not mentioned in the bible, the concept is: Jesus made disciples by inviting 12 men to follow Him, learn from Him, and do life WITH Him. He began with three simple words, "Come with me."

This world needs spiritual fathers and mothers who will follow Jesus' lead and invite others into relationship, into their very lives, with three simple words, "Come with me."

This world needs you.

"Go and make disciples of every nation… Teach these new disciples to obey all the commands I have given you. And be sure of this: I am with you always …" - Jesus

INTRODUCTION

Moses & Joshua. Elijah & Elisha. Joe Montana & Steve Young. Billy Graham & Franklin Graham.

What do these four dynamic duos have in common?

It's pretty evident and strikingly similar: In each of these examples, a great leader passed on his legacy, his mantle, his mission and position to his 'disciple'. But what I find fascinating is the WAY that they passed these things on! They did it through RELATIONSHIP; through Mentoring; through time invested, and through sharing life.

We see this in our culture every day: the medical field calls it a Residency; the business world calls it an Internship; in the trades, you become an Apprentice. The concept is the same: the best way to train someone is to be with them, teaching, coaching, assisting, and assessing; then giving them opportunities to try and fail and try again and learn! I think Jesus is our best example.

I believe Jesus was the Mentor of all Mentors! The Discipler of all Disciplers! I think we can learn all we need to know from His example!

When He chose twelve guys to disciple, *"Jesus went up on a mountainside and called to him those he wanted, and they came to him. He appointed twelve – designating them apostles – **that they might be with him** and that he might send them out to preach and to have authority to drive out demons."* (ie. To carry on his legacy & mission = the Kingdom of God coming to rule in love on the earth!) Mark 3: 14-15

When Jesus made disciples, he didn't just invite them to a six-week class. He didn't toss the Torah to Thomas and tell him to read it. He didn't ask them to write a summary of his last sermon so that when he came back into town they could get together and de-brief. Instead, he said three of the most powerful words to ever be spoken in relationship: *"Come with me,"* Mark 6:31. To Simon and Andrew, he said it this way, *"Come, follow me,"* Mark 1:16.

Jesus didn't just invite them to a lecture or a church service. He invited them to be WITH Him. He invited them into His very life. He invited them to JOIN Him, to learn from Him, to travel with Him, and to KNOW HIM. He invited them into RELATIONSHIP.

I believe with all my heart the old saying, "More is caught than taught." We know that Jesus *taught* his disciples: we have the Gospel accounts full of His teachings. But the twelve chosen disciples got even more than his teachings: they got His friendship, His behind-the-scenes explanations; **they got the Teacher himself.**

Mentoring & Discipling

The terms *Mentoring* and *Discipling* are not synonymous, but in this book I will often use them interchangeably. Technically, Webster's Dictionary defines a **mentor** as "an experienced and trusted advisor." Therefore, mentoring is defined as advising or training someone, especially a younger colleague.

Discipling is simply the process of making disciples. A **disciple** is defined as a follower or one who attaches themselves to the person or beliefs of another. In this book, we are specifically talking about making disciples of Jesus, who, before leaving the earth for heaven, told *His* disciples, *"Go, and make disciples of all nations, baptizing them in the name of the Father and of the Son and of the Holy Spirit. Teach these new disciples to obey all the commands I have given you." Matthew 28: 19-20*

The term "Discipleship" is making a comeback, if you will, in the churches, and I thank God for it! We need to be trained and taught the scriptures, how to live them out in daily connection with Jesus, and how to be led by Holy Spirit. But I believe all this discipling happens BEST in relationship; specifically, mentoring relationships.

"Mentoring," also, is a bit of a buzz word these days! And I think it is great! But mentoring has been more than a buzz word for me: it has become a way of life! I have spent the past thirty years walking alongside young women, college-age young adults, young moms, and pre-marital couples. I have found that the best way to disciple is to invite people into a mentoring relationship. The best way to pass on the teachings of Jesus is to not only study together, but to do life together.

And I've found that the only way to share the love of God with others is to feel the love of God for others. Herein lies the true key to Mentoring and Discipling: it is love. It is first living in and from the love my Father has for me until I am so full that I naturally overflow with His love to others. I must first BE a disciple of Jesus before I can make any. I must first live loved myself, for then I can and will love others with his love.

In my early twenties, I worked for **Youth For Christ/Campus Life**. In one of our trainings they taught us this motto: *"They won't care what you know until they know that you care."* And I have found it to be true. The number one requirement for becoming a mentor or discipling someone is to first love them as Jesus has loved you. Each person is not a project, but a precious child of God.

If you have experienced the love and grace and forgiveness of God for yourself, you are ready to mentor someone else, for you have something to give away. Whether you are hoping to be mentored/discipled or you are interested in learning more about mentoring others, I pray that the stories and examples in this book will encourage you to go for it!

There is no shortage of information in this world; there is a shortage of love. There is no shortage of resources and great teachers; we have podcasts and books and e-books and live-stream.... What we need today is live-*relationship*. Face to face relationships. Close enough to look into another's eyes or hold another's hand. We need hearts that care enough to spend time and invest in the heart of another.

This all began in the heart of our good Father. From heaven, he didn't just send commandments, He sent His Son, who came to BE WITH us, to seek and save the lost, and to love the ones in front of Him. Then the ones in front of Him were so transformed that they naturally turned and loved the ones in front of them. Ripples that began in heaven. Became waves of love that changed the world. One mentoring discipleship relationship at a time.

Going Deeper

1. In the Mentoring Relationships between Moses & Joshua, Elijah & Elisha, Joe Montana & Steve Young . . . what was required from the Mentors (or Disciplers)? What must they have given to the relationship? Make a list.

   _____

   _____

   _____

2. In each of these relationships, what must the Disciples have to have given to the relationship? What did they bring?

   _____

   _____

   _____

3. What was the fruit of these relationships? What happened as a result of all this giving and receiving?

_____ _____

_____

4. Which of the things you listed above do you want to grow in giving? In receiving? Time & Accessibility? Vulnerability? Humility? Wisdom? Knowledge of God's word? Patience? Grace? Honesty? Opportunities to try? To fail? To succeed? Listening to Holy Spirit, or training others to do so?

_____

_____

_____

5. Why would there be more fruitful results in a Mentoring Relationship than in a Discipleship Class? List all you can think of!

_____

_____

_____

_____

_____

_____

CHAPTER 1

ALL FOR JESUS
My Story

"I alone cannot change the world, but I can cast a stone across the waters to create many ripples." – Mother Teresa

I watched the van as it drove away, taking my parents and siblings with it, and leaving me, for the first time in my life, very much alone. I was 18 years old, and had just graduated from high school the night before, surrounded by my family, classmates, and friends. I had never been without my family or friends all around me. I grew up in a close-knit Christian home, and I was the kind of girl who liked home. I never went to summer camp, or girl scout camp, or even church camp. I had never experienced life away from my family or my wonderful friends; I had never experienced being alone.

But when the call came, I knew I would go! It was a dream come true! Earlier that spring, my best friend and I had auditioned for every Live Show of every Amusement Park that we could find. We had dreamed for years of being on stage, singing, dancing, and actually getting paid for it! So, when Cedar Point called and said I had been cast in the Country Gold Show, I was speechless and overjoyed and so excited… I just hadn't counted on being so alone!

I could see my mom's hand out the window as they drove out of sight, still waving, still crying no doubt. I was crying as well. Loneliness descended and enveloped me. What now? I knew no one there, knew nothing about the place; I had never even BEEN to Cedar Point... we were Kings Island and Opry Land kids! I just began walking the park, me and 40,000 other people who were there that day. Yet walking among them in a bit of a haze, I felt very much, desperately alone.

And this was where I discovered the truth: This is where I found out I was never alone. This was when Jesus became real, my closest and dearest friend. I found it is true: not until Jesus is all you have do you discover that Jesus is all you need. And He was. For me.

I would spend my morning hours listening to Amy Grant cassette tapes on my new stereo system I had just gotten for graduation. Then I'd take my pop tart and my carton of milk out to the beach area, read my bible, and pray. How sweet were the ways He spoke to me, comforted me, and made Himself so real. In one encounter, I could see Him in my mind's eye walking toward me on the water, reaching out His hand, and saying, "Peace, be still, Lori. I am right here."

He also graciously answered my prayers - (and my Parents' prayers, I know). Only three days into rehearsals, in which I was starting to get to know my fellow cast members (and starting to understand how very green and inexperienced was this little Christian girl from Indiana), one of our assistant directors quietly said to me, "I heard you are a Christian. We have a Bible Study for Live Shows people... the Pastor who leads it has a son who plays trumpet in the Keystone Cops. We meet on Thursday nights: Would you like to join us? I'll pick you up?"

And that Thursday night was the first of me spending four years of summer Thursday nights in the little home of a quiet Methodist Pastor and his wife, who simply opened their home and invited us in. Pastor Bob was so kind and caring that he never complained about starting at 10:00 p.m. when all the shows were finally done in the park, and we could get off work. Years later, I realized what a sacrifice he and Pat had made for us college kids who needed a home to go to, a family to belong to, and a teacher to guide us.

Pastor Bob loved to worship, and since we were all singers and musicians, you can imagine how we filled those nights with songs of praise. I remember the first night hearing those around me lift their voices; I had been a little nervous, not knowing a soul there except Bill who invited me. But when the singing began, "How can I give thanks for the things You have done for me? Things so undeserved, yet you did to prove your love for me…" I opened my eyes, the tears starting to fall, and thought, "Oh! You know Him, too? You must love Him as I do! He must have been there for you as He has been for me! I feel like I've come home!!!!" For Jesus was truly there.

Pastor Bob would open the Word of God and teach us, and we were hungry for every morsel he fed us. We would talk and discuss and pray into the wee hours of the morning, and sometimes take it down the road to Perkins Pancake House, since they were open 24/7.

One night, Pastor Bob led us in prayer, and asked us to imagine Jesus standing in front of us. "First look at his feet, see his sandals, then his robe, then look up into His face. See Jesus placing His hand upon your head, and hear Him speak to you, 'Peace I leave with you. My peace I give to you…,'" and I felt the presence of Jesus touch my head and descend down upon me and envelope me. And this time, instead of loneliness, I was filled with His own Spirit, His love, His peace and joy. And I have never been the same. My once anxious heart began to live differently, and everywhere I went, I invited others to come know and experience this Jesus who was everything good and everything I needed. I wanted them to know Him, too.

Because one man and his wife opened their home and their hearts, and laid down their lives and their good nights' sleep, 12-15 of us lonely college kids became family, became disciples, became passionate about making disciples for the Jesus whom we loved.

My fourth and last summer at Cedar Point, I became a Vocal Supervisor, so I rehearsed and worked with every vocalist in the park. And like my Supervisor had done for me my first year, I would quietly speak to each one, "Hey, we have a group of Live Shows people that meets for Bible Study, fellowship, and worshiping Jesus on Thursday nights! Would you like to come try it? I'll pick you up?" After a while, they saw me coming and knew what I would be asking! But I was not deterred! I loved them and had long conversations with them, especially my atheist friends, and I continued to invite!

I'll never forget that last summer as long as I live: within the first month, we had so many young adults packing Pastor Bob's little house that they were sitting on the floor, in the kitchen, and up the stairs! One invitation four years earlier sparked many invitations over the next years, and multiplied, like ripples in a lake.

This is a book on Discipling through Mentoring Relationships. *But the most important part of this book is the why.* **It's all for Jesus**. It's all I ever want to do. It's because He swallowed up my loneliness forever, as Melissa Helser says, when he came in to be one with me by His wonderful abiding Spirit. He will never leave me nor forsake me. In fact, He has invited me to be One with Him. Forever.

Through mentoring and discipling from a humble pastor in Sandusky, OH, the disciples he and Pat made that summer have multiplied across the country, telling others, mentoring many, and making disciples all across the world. It began in a small home with one invitation like a pebble thrown into a quiet pond; and the ripple effect of heaven began.

We can change the world. I truly believe it. One discipleship relationship at a time.

"All the believers devoted themselves to the apostle's teaching, and to fellowship, and to sharing in meals, and to prayer. . . They broke bread in their homes and ate together with glad and sincere hearts, praising God and enjoying the favor of all the people. And the Lord added to their number daily those who were being saved." Acts 2:42-47

Going Deeper

1. Have you ever experienced loneliness that enveloped you, whether alone or in crowds of people? Describe how this felt and why.

    _____

    _____

2. Do you still experience loneliness? Or what happened in your life to help bring you into 'family' or relationship?

    _____

    _____

3. As we discuss mentoring relationships, do you find your heart longing to have a Mentor? Ask God to begin to speak to you and lead you to one.

    _____

    _____

4. Last, ask our good Father if there is someone in your life who might feel this kind of loneliness and be in need of someone to just invite them to … get coffee, your small group, or to a meal at your home? One invitation can change the course of a person's life! Ask and listen and write those names here: _____!

CHAPTER 2

QUALIFICATIONS OF A MENTOR

Natalie's Story

"Being mentored was the single most impressionable thing in my life… It's shaped me into the woman of God I am today!"
- Natalie

Let's get the big question out of the way first: can anyone be a Mentor? What qualifications are required?

Let's start with what it doesn't require: Being a mentor does NOT require a Seminary degree! It does not require a knowledge of the entire Bible or an answer to every theological question! And it doesn't require you to have your act together or be living a perfect life before you can become a Mentor! (Feeling better yet?)

Natalie was a squirrelly sixth grader in my very first general music class, my very first year of teaching. It's not that she was any more squirrelly than the rest; ALL sixth graders are pretty squirrelly! Natalie just talked more and faster than the rest, so I could more readily see and hear from her that working with sixth graders would be, shall we say, a unique challenge and adventure!

I remember standing in front of this first class of mine, looking at them as they were *not* looking at me, and wondering how in the world I could bring the noise level down to one in which I could actually speak. Day after day, I tried different approaches and quickly learned: I was in over my head! They weren't too interested in general music, even in general. They didn't respond too well to my strict and stern voice that I had been encouraged by some professors to use in the first few weeks to 'establish who was in charge.' And even just 'waiting on them to quiet down' was futile; I was feeling quite hopeless. Music I knew: sixth graders I did not.

One noisy day, in complete frustration, I just casually and rather sarcastically said, "So can I tell you about my dog?" To my complete surprise, a few heads turned my way. Natalie, first always to speak, said at rapid-fire pace, "You have a dog?"

Wow. Someone had listened! So, I continued, "Yes, Christy our Sheltie was my husband's dog for the past 12 years, and now she lives with us since we were married last April..." *"You are MARRIED?" she interrupted.* "Yes, just a few months ago, we ...." *"What's your husband's name? What's your DOG'S name? Do you have pictures?"*

As more kids began to listen, I was thinking, "What is happening? They are more interested in knowing about ME than about music... hmmm..." So, I tried to keep it going, "Yes, this weekend, our poor dog got lost." Now I had ALL heads turn my way! ('Cause who doesn't love a dog?). "What happened?" Natalie asked breathlessly.

"We couldn't find her, and we were starting to be really worried. Then I remembered we had a creek down behind our house, and I started running...." (At this point, I had the attention of every student in the room... this wasn't lost on me....). Natalie had moved to the literal edge of her seat.

"So, I ran down the back yard to the creek, looked up and down, and THERE... there she was, stuck between a log and the bank, unable to move her paws or climb back out....." "OH NO!" they all cried. (Maybe teaching sixth graders wasn't completely impossible . . .)

"We got her out. My husband pulled and . . ." and I told them the whole story while they listened with rapt attention. When I finished, I naturally asked, "Do any of you have a dog?" And nearly every hand went up in the air, and every voice seemed to say, "I do! I do!" So, to maintain control, I had them take turns. And now, they were all willing to listen to the other speak, for each of them had a story to tell. And I let them tell it.

And the next day, we had something to ask about, "How's your dog? Feeling better?" At the time, I didn't understand how this was going to translate into being able to teach them about music; but looking back, I see it clearly now. The old adage is beyond true: *"They won't care what you know until they know that you care."* Once they realized I actually cared about them and their lives and their dogs and their baby brothers and their parents, they cared about what I knew and said as well. They even began to care about music, because they knew I cared about them.

And thus began a new revelation not only about teaching, but about having any influence at all: **relationship is the key**. Getting to know these students as real people endeared them to me. I not only began to care about them, I actually began to enjoy them! (Ok, well, most of the time!) I think they could tell; people usually can.

I had accepted this teaching position because the permanent teacher was on maternity leave. I had gotten to know her because I was volunteering as a leader with Youth For Christ and their ministry in the public schools called Campus Life. I didn't even want to teach music, or so I thought. I just showed up to Campus Life because I wanted to teach kids about JESUS. Living in a new city as a newlywed, I had asked God how I could do this? Then, in a highly spiritual moment of revelation, proceeded to open the phone book to YOUTH and found YOUTH FOR CHRIST. (Pretty deep, I know). The club met before school, and it happened to meet in the music teachers' room. The very first day I walked in, both music teachers looked at each other, then looked at me, and said, "Yes!! We've been praying for you! You can take Deb's place when she goes on Maternity leave!"

"Um, no, thank you! I know I have a degree in music, but I just want to talk to kids about Jesus."

"Uh huh. Ok. Well, we know why you're here. We've been praying for a Christian music teacher to take Deb's place! We prayed you here!"

The principal called and offered me the job. I told him no. A few weeks later he called again, and I said, "No, thank you!" When Deb went on leave, they hired someone else, but, unfortunately, they let her go after a week. (Maybe she didn't know about the whole 'dog conversation' trick....)

The third time he called I said to God, "God! I know I told you I'd go wherever you wanted me to go and do whatever you wanted me to do~ But Father! I really don't want to teach school~!" *"You want to tell kids about me, Lori?"* "You know I do, Jesus!" *"Then this is my door into their lives, into their hearts, into loving them. This is my answer to your request."*

And I said yes.

And at 24 years of age, I began to learn that Father truly does know best. His ways are always higher and better than our ideas and plans! I found out that I would not only be teaching music, I also had lunch-room duty!! YAY! (That was sarcasm, in case you didn't know; this was possibly my worst nightmare.) But again, God knew best. Guess what I could do during lunch? Walk around and talk to students!! Sit and get to know them better. Listen. Listening is really big. I really began to care.

Then I began to invite. I told every class I had about Campus Life, that we met on Thursday mornings, and that if they came before school, we would play fun games and eat free donuts!!! I reminded them every day! (It's amazing how free you can be when you don't really care whether you keep your job or not!) Our numbers began to grow. We went from having around 20 students each Thursday morning at 7:00 am to having over 80!!

Guess who came? Natalie. And Natalie not only came, she brought her friends. And they came to our Retreat, and they gave their lives to Jesus. And I saw again how relationship proceeds making disciples.

Natalie eventually went on to high school. I went on to work on staff for YFC. But the relationships I made never moved on, they moved deeper! I began to meet with Natalie and her friends AFTER school. We would go get ice cream. They got to ride in my car. Riding in my car was a very big thing. (with parents' permission of course!) I asked them if they'd like to keep growing in their relationship with Jesus and maybe meet for a bible study once a week. They said yes.

I began to disciple Natalie and Rashida and Courtney and Lindsay through Mentoring Relationships! **As you will see in this book, I'm a big fan of doing this in small groups** because the relationship they have is not just with me, but with each other; and then we had built a community, a small family, a 'place to belong' as we grew to love and know Jesus in the most beautiful ways. Eventually more of their friends wanted to come, so we had times for them, too.

I also formed other mentoring groups with students I had gotten to know while teaching music. One of these groups intentionally decided to NOT invite their Christian friends, but only to invite their friends who didn't know Jesus yet! We named that group The Perpetual Ceiling Fans ('cause remember 6th – 9th graders are a bit squirrelly), and we invited kids to come talk about their views on life, religion, and friendships. This group made a space where the Christian kids naturally ended up sharing their faith just by answering the questions that we discussed; and at least 5-6 kids said yes to Jesus that year! But first they said yes to relationship: to being known and being heard and being truly cared about.

Let me be clear: I had no idea what I was doing. Remember, this was the question at the beginning of this chapter: what qualifications must you have to be a Mentor? I found there really are only two: **Love Jesus and love his people.** That's pretty much it. I learned how important it is to really care, to be in people's everyday lives, and to really listen. I learned how to ask questions to get others to talk about their lives, what they believed, and how they felt about things. But these things I learned by simply saying yes to God and yes to being in relationship and yes to a job that **He** led me to so that I could make relationships before I made Disciples.

And Natalie? Today, Natalie lives in Nashville, TN with her husband and four beautiful kids. I can tell you she helps lead women's bible studies at her church, and she has a real heart to help women connect in relationships. I can tell you we don't get to see each other very often, though we did get to meet up last week when they were in Indiana visiting family. We don't connect every week, but I am elated that we stay in touch! And guess who was the first person I asked to give me feedback on the importance of Mentoring Relationships?

You see, God had gone to great lengths to get Natalie to a sixth-grade music class in Carmel, Indiana, where she could meet an inexperienced music teacher who knew very little about mentoring her.

Natalie's Story

Natalie was born in Iran. She was left as a tiny baby on the steps of a Mosque in Tehran, orphaned at 5 days old. Here's Natalie's story in her own words:

"My parents were over in Tehran because my dad was working for Ross Perot. They didn't have any kids, and decided to adopt. Their landlord told them his son worked at the hospital and there were some babies that needed homes. They went and picked me when I was five and a half months old. This was July of 1978. The Shah was leaving Iran and all

Americans needed to evacuate. In the hustle and confusion, my adoption papers were stolen, with my dad's briefcase, so they had to smuggle me out of the country. They made it out, and I was issued a passport in Turkey, from where we then made safe passage to the states. I became an American citizen when I was five!"

"Though I was raised in the Methodist church, I didn't really get it till I was in Campus Life. I loved those times you would take us out for ice cream after school. Then we met at that Quaker church for bible study while we were in high school! When college hit, we had that Bible study at your church, remember? I loved those times with you and those girls…"

Yes, even when they went to college, we would continue to meet throughout the summers that they were home! Every other week we would go downtown in Indianapolis to the Children's Home and read bed-time stories to the kids whose parents were in jail or gone or unable to care for them; some who had become orphans.

What a full circle God had in mind for the orphan from Iran who came to know Jesus. What a ripple effect happens when we listen and love and invite into relationship, so that others can know this Jesus who did not leave any of us as orphans, but came to be with us, by His Spirit, to live inside of us so that none of us would ever have to be alone ever again.

You don't need a master's degree in theology to be a Mentor for Jesus. You just have to love the one in front of you that God highlights, be patient if they seem to not be listening, and maybe start by asking them about their dog.

"I will not leave you as orphans; I will come to you." John 14: 18

"Go and make disciples of every nation, … teaching them to obey everything I have commanded you. And surely I am with you always, to the very end of the age." Matthew 28:19-20

GOING DEEPER

1. Have you ever tried to 'witness' for Jesus and felt like the person wasn't listening or that the conversation wasn't going anywhere? What questions could you ask about THEM... their family life, background, hobbies, home town... In order to get to know them and begin relationship? Don't forget to ask them about their dog!

    When you think of these people who need to meet Jesus, do you start with caring? What would it look like to LOVE them where they are without trying to change them? Start by asking Holy Spirit to fill you with HIS love for them, and eyes to see them the way He does!

    Father, what are some practical and fun ways I could LOVE this person, encourage them? Write any random thoughts that come to mind: _____

    _____

    _____

2. Have you ever felt 'stuck' in a job or season that you didn't enjoy, hoping to get out as soon as possible? Ask God today to show you WHY you might be there for this time, for these people, for His purposes? Ask Him to show you HOW you can invest in the lives around you by asking questions, caring, and being His love to the people around you? Ask Him to give you a new perspective on this job and season you are in. What is He saying?

    _____

    _____

    _____

    _____

    _____

    _____

CHAPTER 3

SHARE YOUR LIFE
The Trio Story

"With a mother's love and affectionate attachment to you, we were happy to share with you not only the gospel of God but also our lives – because you had become so dear to us."
I Thessalonians 2: 8

"Through mentoring relationships, I learned of God's commitment to doing all of life with me. His love is not just for a big encounter moment, He is in it for all of life – the transitions, silly moments, meal moments, …as well as the big life-changing encounters."
- Nancy

"Miss Lori! It isn't fair! Can you believe that girl said that?" and I walked in to the little room in our church to find two sweet seventh graders comforting a third who was crying and obviously upset, which I'd come to find out was a pretty normal day in the life of a seventh grader.

"What's up, girls? How can I help?" We had just finished a rehearsal for our KidStuf program at church where these teenage girls were part of our worship team that led the younger ones in worship-choreography and dance. "It isn't fair! What can we do?" they cried in sad, whining voices, which I'd come to find out was a pretty normal voice in the life of a seventh grader!

It was so long ago, I don't remember exactly the scenario that had hurt young Nancy's feelings; but I remember the way her friends Sarah and Erin were there for her. And I remember I said something about, "Well, let's look at what God might say about it..." and we looked up a scripture that came to my mind.

"Wow. That's perfect," one of them said. "That reminds me of that verse in Ephesians I just memorized," said the other, and so we turned and read that one together too. "OH MY GOODNESS!" another said. "This is AMAZING! It's almost like - like God is *TALKING TO US!*"

And I smiled, and agreed that He was, and we prayed; and we all felt Him there. "This was so good," they said. " Could we do this again next week after rehearsal?"

And I smiled and thought, "Um, yes? Meet together and study God's word and bring Him our cares and listen for His loving voice?" Ummm. YES! SIGN ME UP!

And we did. We met the next week, and again the following. And we kept meeting, and sharing, and studying God's word, and praying, and some crying... week after week; then year after year. And that was over 16 years ago; we just never stopped. Though we live in different cities, we keep sharing life!

The Trio, as I affectionately call them, has been an unexpected blessing of unspeakable joy in my life. This Mentoring Relationship, MLo and the Trio – as we like to call ourselves – has lasted over sixteen years. Not all mentoring relationships go this way!! In fact, MOST don't. But this one has been different.

Why? Well, partly because we seem to have 'clicked' organically, and God knit our hearts together pretty early on to really love and care for each other; we genuinely enjoy being together. And maybe partly because these girls came from amazing Christian homes where they grew up knowing Jesus alongside our boys at our church. But the biggest reason I believe these amazing young ladies are still in deep relationship with me and each other after all these years is simply this: they made an intentional covenant decision to do so.

The Trio has learned about covenant relationships by BEING in covenant relationships! We have not continued to meet because we always got along, always agreed, or always walked the straight & narrow! We've continued to meet because we have learned that true Jesus-like relationships work through the angry conflicts, talk it through when we are hurt or offended, and continue to believe in each other even when one of us may not believe in ourselves! These girls have lived it and learned: we truly need each other. We were not designed to do life alone.

In Erin's Words

This mentoring group has truly become family. I don't have words to adequately express the impact they've had on me. Our commitment to love, encourage, challenge, and stand beside one another is a gift that I will forever be thankful for. There were seasons when relationship was not easy, but it was always worth it. We are now hundreds of miles away from each other, but we have seen the fruit of sacrificial, committed love, rooted in Jesus, and so we are committed still. When our dear friend and mentor, Miss Lori, took a group of middle school girls under her wing, I'm not sure that any of us knew how much it would shape our lives. Now, after years full of road trips, graduations, first loves, weddings, new babies, job changes, countless tears and even more joyful moments, here we are still, stirring each other on to live connected to The Vine. It is my great hope that I could be to someone else half the mentor that mine has been to me.

Jesus' Example

When Jesus invited 12 men to simply, "Come with Me," He invited them into his very life. He invited them to follow Him wherever He went and whatever He was doing. Therefore, these 12 men were discipled in the context of family and the context of everyday life.

Think about it. They began to really KNOW this Jesus. They not only learned the ways of the Kingdom and the meanings of His parables, they also learned about the Man himself. They learned that He was the same yesterday and today that He had been last month; in front of crowds or when they were alone; Jesus showed them an authentic life of joy and peace no matter what was going on. They learned that He didn't just preach on prayer, He actually practiced it, and talked with His Father early in the morning as well as throughout His day. They must have learned what kinds of food were his favorites, what made Him laugh, and what brought Him to tears.

They knew what it was like to be encouraged by Him, "Blessed are you, Peter, for flesh and blood has not revealed this to you, but only my Father …"; and they knew what it was like to be rebuked, "Get thee behind me, Satan, for you do not have in mind the things of God, but the things of man." They knew the conviction that came upon them while they were arguing about who was the greatest, and He simply pulled a child up on His lap and lovingly reminded them that the Kingdom belongs to such as these. They could receive His correction because they knew His commitment to them. They could receive His discipline because they knew of His unconditional love for them. Out of relationship, they learned He could be trusted, and in the end, they gave it all for Him as He had done for them.

But they not only were in relationship with Jesus, they were in constant relationship with each other. I believe Jesus intentionally modeled the best method of discipleship in GROUPS, for in order to learn how to "love one another," there had to be a "one another." In order to learn the love that the Father, Son, and Holy Spirit share in community, there has to be 'another.' Jesus could have met with Peter alone, John alone, James alone, but instead, He wanted them to learn to LOVE in the context of family – in tension, in conflict, in great joy and shared celebration! When Peter was being prideful, I bet Matthew called him out on it! When James let his temper get the best of him, I'm sure he and John had to learn to forgive and reconcile. They knew when Philip came in with that look on his face, that he had done that thing again! They knew which ones snored, which ones told the best jokes, and which ones you didn't want to talk to before they had had their morning coffee!

In relationship, their 'stuff' came to light, and the Light of the world was there to shine some truth on it! In the presence of perfect love, imperfections were clearly seen; in the presence of perfect patience, their impatience became something they wanted to be free of. Jesus, the Truth, was like a holy Mirror that walked around with them revealing Truth, and revealing when they were not walking in their true selves. The presence of Truth set them free!

And so it is with Mentors. Though FAR from perfect, I knew my role was to simply hold up Truth like a mirror to the Trio, so they could see for themselves if they were walking in it or not! Without having to point out their sins, I learned to point out who God had made them to be, and Holy Spirit did the rest.

I learned that to mentor like Jesus meant inviting The Trio into my very life; to see not only the ways I followed and loved Him, but also the ways in which I missed it sometimes, SO that they could see the ways I needed Him, ran to Him, and received His cleansing. I shared with them my failures as well as my victories, and I shared the process I was currently learning in the meantime. They quickly learned I was not perfect, but hopefully that I was perfectly committed to Jesus and dependent on Him for everything.

When the Trio first started to meet, we did simple Bible Studies once a week. But then I began to invite them to go with me to pick up one of my boys from basketball practice. "Wanna ride in the convertible?" always got a yes! "Wanna stop for ice cream on the way home?" And eventually, "Wanna go across the street to the nursing home and sing Christmas carols for the residents? Wanna pray for them as we go?" And we began to really DO LIFE together.

We celebrated birthdays and began to keep track of the prophetic words spoken over each other, reminding each other what FATHER said about them, especially when they couldn't remember! We cried during sad times, laughed a lot during the happy, and were there for each other when needed. We took long walks, served together at church, and worshiped with just the four of us in my back yard.

When one went out of town for college, we helped move her in, cried with her parents, and learned about 'group chats' in text messaging. When one moved out of state to train with Youth With a Mission (YWAM), we had a going-away party with all the families, for we had all become one big family by this time! More than once, Nancy and I drove 5 hours to Nashville, TN to take Erin out to lunch, hug her neck, and then drove back home!

Road trips became like a favorite thing! Erin and I drove 2 hours to Bloomington to encourage Sarah in her pledge season of sorority. And when Sarah went to grad school in St. Louis, Nancy and I drove the 6 or 7 hours to be in her world, see where she would be, and pray with our friend. During those road trips, someone would put on a worship song, and we'd invite Jesus to be among us. Someone else would say, "Miss Lori, have you ever read Romans 8 in The Message? Oh! Listen to this!" And as she read, Holy Spirit began to speak, His presence was so near, and literal tears were streaming down our faces. (There were many times on road trips, I probably should've pulled over as Holy Spirit filled the car and brought us to tears of adoration and wonder.)

Life together. This is not only Jesus' WAY of discipling, it is His GIFT. You and I and every person on the planet were all designed to do life together, in community, knowing others and being known. This is relationship. We were not designed to do life alone.

Last night on the news, in the wake of two more mass shootings in the U.S. this past weekend, I heard these statistics: The top three commonalities between these troubled shooters over the past 10 years are consistently listed as **isolation, loneliness, and lack of support or connection.** 27% of Millennials say they have no close friends. 23% said they had no acquaintances at all.

I believe that every life, every person is of utmost value to our Heavenly Father. And I believe His heart breaks each time one of his little lambs wanders off and is lost and alone. I believe one reason He sent Holy Spirit to be our constant Comforter, Helper, and Friend was so that no one, at any time, would ever have to be alone ever again. It's time for us to introduce Him to those who need Him.

Instead of becoming overwhelmed by statistics, I believe there's something you and I can do, right now, today. There are lonely people all around us. They may wear business suits or work-out clothes or teach your child's second grade class. They may be standing next to you in the grocery line or sitting next to you in the pew. You may not even recognize them as lonely, but Father knows. What if everyone reading these words right now were to mentor just one person this year, inviting them into relationship, or just to go get coffee? What if each of us asked God to open our eyes and our hearts to truly see what He sees and feel what He feels when we encounter one who is lost in loneliness? What if we just asked, "How are you?" and then sat down long enough to listen and really care?

GOING DEEPER

1. If God is stirring in your heart right now what He feels in His, let's ask Him to speak to us. In the remaining chapters of this book, I'll be giving you more specific and helpful how-to's and steps to take in this mentoring adventure. For now, would you take a minute and ask God, "Father, you see the lonely and hurting around me. Would you bring to my mind right now one or two or three persons that really need a friend, a listening ear, and maybe a mentor to do life with them?"

    Now, would you wait and listen. Then write down who or what comes to your mind. _____

    _____

    _____

    _____

2. Next steps? Maybe give that person a call or text, or get to know them at the next soccer game. We'll talk more about how to know when the time and person is right in later chapters, but for now, someone may need a friend today. You may be the answer to someone's prayer for help. You could just invite them to sit with you at the game or to ride along to the next one. Jesus' words still do just fine: "Come with me." Write a practical action step here:

    _____

    _____

    _____

    _____

    The world needs you. You have something to share. Share your very life.

    We were not meant to do life alone. We were designed to do life together.

"This is not the time to pull away and neglect meeting together, as some have formed the habit of doing. In fact, we should come together even more frequently, eager to encourage and urge each other onward . . ." Hebrews 10:25 TPT

CHAPTER 4

WHERE TO START
Morgan's Story

*"I do not come from a family of faith, so mentoring has helped
me in many ways… It has been such a joy to learn from women
who are in the next stage of life. To hear their stories, see how they
handled situations, and learn from their encounters with Jesus…"*
- Morgan

Let's get practical. Let's say you're open to becoming a Mentor, but
you don't know where to start. In the next few chapters we will touch on
questions like:

How do I effectively disciple someone in a mentoring relationship?

What materials or resources should I use?

When do you know it's a fit, and what if it's not?

Whom should I choose to mentor/disciple?

Where do I even start?

Where To Start

If your heart is stirred and you are catching the vision that Jesus
cast for us, you are ready. We truly CAN change the world one mentoring
discipleship relationship at a time.

The first step is simply to BE a disciple. Talk to the Father who longs for all to belong and be in relationship. Offer yourself in surrender to be available to mentor whomever He brings to your life. Spend time with Jesus, the Vine, and connect to Him as a branch, learning to abide and remain and find your source of life in Him. This is His design and how He wants to bear fruit through you. In the same way that a branch does not "do" anything to produce fruit (except remain connected to the Vine), we do not need to strive to 'produce' disciples, but simply let the sap of His Spirit flow through us and work with us to accomplish any good work! Take a deep breath! All pressure is off! Mentoring, and all of our lives in Jesus, will flow naturally as we remain in His love and allow Him to do the work. If at any point, you feel yourself striving or the pressure of 'making' disciples, stop and surrender again to His Spirit at work in and through you! It will require sacrifice, but there is no striving in the Kingdom! This should be fun!!

Whom To Mentor

Next, begin to ask God whom to start with. One way that God has led me to know whom He wanted me to mentor can be summed up in these three practical things to look for:

Highlighted, Hungry, and Heart Connection

1. **Highlighted:** Often God will 'highlight' someone to me, meaning they stick out to me, I notice them in a crowd, or He keeps bringing this person to mind and I wonder about their walk with Jesus. Sometimes, it's someone that God has obviously brought into my life, they have ASKED me to mentor them, or it could be someone I just keep running into over and over. I pay attention to whom He highlights.

2. **Hungry:** Next, I will try to get to know this person in an informal way, just stopping to chat, or maybe inviting them out for coffee

just for fun. I'm now looking for Hunger: do I sense a real desire to grow in Jesus? Do they ask questions of me or about Jesus or His word? Whether they're a believer yet or not, are they open to talking about their faith journey, open to learning new things, and humble enough to be teachable? Do they seem to be willing to invest the time? Do they show up?

3. **Heart Connection:** Do we seem to click? Though getting to know anyone can have its awkward moments, does the conversation begin to flow? Is there a two-way dialogue and an ease in being together? Sometimes, God asks us to just be obedient and pour into people whom we don't have much in common with; this is valid. But for a true mentoring relationship, I believe there needs to be enough of an organic connection that it doesn't feel forced. Remember, this kind of discipling is a mentoring RELATIONSHIP, and the most important part is to truly love and care for the ones God calls us to.

Is It a Good Fit?

If there's not really a connection, it's ok to recognize that. If we've just met for coffee once or twice, I often will bless them and leave it at that. If they have specifically asked me to mentor them, it is so kind to be clear. Often I will say, "I'm so honored that you would ask me. I'm not able to meet consistently with you during this season, but I love that you are wanting a mentor, and I'd be glad to suggest some people you might really click with and enjoy. In the meantime, I'd love to connect every now and then and just see how you are doing!"

If there IS a heart connection, and I sense a sincere hunger to learn and be teachable, I might ask if they'd be interested in doing a bible study or reading through a book with me for the next 6 weeks. This is a great first step in discipling because it has a beginning and an ending, which is really helpful during this early stage. (Also, I often will invite in groups of 3-4… more on this later!)

Meaning, if the 6-week study goes well, they seem to be intentional and give of their time and commitment, and if God seems to be blessing our times together, then I may invite them into more! How do I know if God is blessing it? I'll write more on this later, but if I see real growth, real willingness to obey Holy Spirit's guidance and leadership, or simply feel His presence strongly when we're together, I know He is in it! In the next chapter, we'll talk more about what this looks like & how to measure & discern if we are accomplishing our goal.

And if, at the end of the 6 weeks, it's apparent it's not a good fit, then I can bless them and encourage them and thank them for going through it with me! Again, I always offer to connect or be available if they ever want to talk about something we've touched on, and I truly try to check in on these new friends every now and then!

What Materials or Curriculum Do I Use?

First, to become a disciple of Jesus, the Bible is our foundation. Sometimes we will read through a book of the bible together, sometimes do a more in-depth workbook study. (We girls love a good Beth Moore or Pricilla Shirer study! My husband prefers topical studies with his guys like Marketplace ministry, or bibilical teachings on finances or Leadership in the Kingdom. And guys, my husband also enjoys discussing these things while doing a project together … working on something side-by-side). Or, we might do a topical study on subjects like forgiveness, prayer, or the gifts of the Spirit, to name a few. Sometimes the church you go to will have a Discipleship Curriculum that you can follow. But even then, the most important answer to "What materials do I use?" is :

Whatever they need! This is another advantage of a Mentoring RELATIONSHIP when discipling someone: We must know the person enough to know where they are in their faith journey with Jesus, what

THEY are wanting to grow in, and what do you see that they need at this time in their life? A Discipleship Class is always good, but it cannot adapt its weekly curriculum to the needs of all the students. The curriculum may be studying Ephesians 2 and what it means to be saved by grace, but the student may be in the midst of a marriage collapse and needs to know how the Gospel speaks to forgiveness and reconciliation. THAT student needs a mentor, a friend, a listening ear that can ALSO point them to the Gospel. This is why I am passionate about the RELATIONAL aspect... we must know and be in the lives of those we mentor enough to know what God is doing and saying for each one at that time.

For example, I was leading a group of high school girls through a study on 2 Corinthians. It was great, but I happened to know that at least one of them was asking a lot of questions about a boy and dating and 'how do you know if you should date them,' and ... You guessed it. We took the next two weeks and just studied what the bible has to say about dating and relationships! You can bet their interest in coming increased dramatically! There was a lot of note-taking that week! THIS is where they were and what they needed!

Another woman I had the privilege of discipling had just become a brand new believer with very little knowledge of the Bible or Jesus at all! So, a dear friend of mine joined me as we led Louisa through the Gospel of John, slowly, chapter by chapter, beginning with, "This is where the book of John is found. This is how we find chapter and verse. This is who John was and why he wrote this account of Jesus' life!" THIS is where Louisa was, and what she was needing and wanting to know! And THIS is what makes mentoring and discipling so fun and such a blessing... to introduce people to our wonderful Jesus is the most precious privilege we could have!!!

"For the Son of Man came to seek and save those who are lost."
Luke 19: 10

Morgan's Story

"Mentoring has made such a drastic impact in my life. I do not come from a family of faith, so mentoring has helped me in many ways. My two mentors and the women in my group help bring perspective, challenge me, inspire me, and so much more. When I originally said that I wanted to be mentored I was not sure what that would look like. Do I need to prepare? Do I need to be worried? Should I be super open and risk scaring them away? Should I hold back and not let them truly help me? All of these questions were going through my head the minute I agreed to be a part of this group.

Quickly I realized that all I really had to bring to the table was myself… the good, the bad, and the ugly, and they loved me as I was. I learned I needed to be open to challenge and have a willing heart to hear and implement change in my life. I could not be afraid to open up the darker parts of my story and be 'exposed' to other believers in the Kingdom. This group has given me unconditional love and so much joy. Aside from spiritual growth, and learning to walk a better walk with Jesus, this group has brought me to tears and laughter so many times. We celebrate together. We cry together. We do life together. I would not want it any other way.

Navigating the waters of life can be challenging at times, but God has given me this mentoring group as a life preserver to help me get through. A life preserver can deflate, but if you continue to put air into it, it will fill back up. This is how I feel about mentoring. These women are like the pump helping to refill the air in my floaty whenever I run out … but notice that they are not the preserver themselves… Jesus is! He will ultimately save me, but he gave us one another to help go through this life with… He did not want us to do it alone. I still have to swim and be willing to partner with him, but I don't have to do it alone!

GOING DEEPER

1. Ask Father again, "Whom have you highlighted to me and keep bringing to my mind? How can I casually get to know him or her?

   _____

   _____

2. Is this person hungry, Father? Is it the right time? What have I noticed about their interest, hunger, humility, teachability?"

   _____

   _____

3. What is a first step you could take? Invite for coffee? Invite to small group? Invite for dinner? ESPECIALLY look for those who don't know Jesus yet!

   _____

   _____

4. Does this person seem to have 'buddies', friends who might also enjoy a mentoring group and might make it more fun to do together? Or other men or women this person might enjoy getting to know?

   _____

   _____

5. Guys, is there a current project like mulching, painting, or moving someone that you guys could do together in order to get to know someone as you work?

   _____

   _____

6. Is there someone you've been meeting with but find that each meeting seems fruitless, or emotionally draining because you're trying so hard? Is this someone you could bless and conclude meeting with in an honoring way, always keeping the door open to reconnect in a few months and see how they are doing? Is there another mentor or group you could recommend for them?

CHAPTER 5

WHOM TO MENTOR
Ashlie's Story

"Having a mentor ... means having another person in your life who walks alongside you and allows you to feel seen, loved, valued, and heard... It means having someone who can speak Truth over your life and declare God's goodness, to remind you who you are in Christ." - Ashlie

Let's talk more about whom you should mentor.

The first and easy answer is, "Ask God!" And I've learned that when I ask, I actually need to wait in His presence and listen! Sometimes a face or a name will just flash across my mind, and I know I should at least check it out!

Other times, after asking God in prayer, I journal any thoughts I may be having, people's names, and then I keep my eyes open as I go through my day! Having just asked my Father, who loves to answer when we call, I can trust that He will be speaking and leading me with great joy if I keep my eyes and ears open to what He is doing around me throughout my day!

During one season, I had a few high school girls who were on my heart, and I wondered if it were a good time to invite them into mentoring & discipleship. These young ladies I did not know as well, and I remember thinking they may not be interested, they really didn't know each other, and maybe I had enough going on anyway. I've learned enough over the years that I can ask my good Father, and He will be faithful to lead me! This time, he really did!

I had just recently prayed and asked about inviting these girls. The following Sunday I was walking through the lobby of our church and a woman I had never seen before approached me. She said, "You are a sower." I stopped, looked at her, and asked, "What did you say?" She said it again, "I sense you are a sower of seeds. And you know, in the word of God, the seed IS the word of God. You are a teacher of God's word, and God says sow your seeds…."

I knew it was Him. I knew He was kind enough to encourage me and give me His go ahead for that time! So that season I invited 5 or 6 girls from 2 or 3 different schools to meet once a week for bible study and prayer.

Have you ever been to a first meeting of something when it's a bit awkward and so quiet you could hear a pin drop? That was this group at first! I found that asking general questions was not going to work with these sweet girls; they were going to need me to pull some things out of them! Again, none of this is possible without prayer and the leading of Holy Spirit, so even in the awkwardness, I tried to listen for His wisdom, His ideas… (ok, my prayer was actually, 'HELP, God!')!! And I began to learn how to ask specific questions that EVERY one could answer, and then go around the circle so that each of them KNEW their time was coming and they would be called upon. This may seem elementary, but it can be a huge secret tool in getting quiet ones to open up. (This applies to adults as much as teens!) Something about calling their name and asking them directly frees them up to begin sharing (and helps immensely with the deafening silence issues!)

Simple questions, like "Who is your best friend and why?" or "Describe your favorite pet and why?" are easy access questions based on things that MOST ALL people can relate to. These kinds of questions are HUGE when you are wondering what they are thinking, and if they even want to be there!

Simple key #2: Don't take their lack of response nor the looks on their faces at 'face value!' More often than not, there's more going on than you would ever guess!

Ashlie was in this group. Ashlie has the sweetest smile and the kindest 'presence' about her. But Ashlie the tenth grader was incredibly quiet! I don't believe she spoke more than two words the first few months, she never 'jumped in' or offered to answer any questions, unless she was asked! I initially thought she must be miserable since she had nothing to say; but over the years I learned you truly cannot judge a book by its cover, nor a heart by its facial expressions!

I learned from Ashlie that some hearts are longing and learning and have deeper wells than we would ever believe. I also learned that Ashlie COMING was her way of speaking, and Ashlie CAME more faithfully than any of the rest!

It has been many years since that little group met and went through a bible study together. I'd like to tell you that I was such a motivational mentor that Ashlie eventually loosened up and shared freely with the group. But really, she never did. I loved her faithfulness, her sweetness, her sincerity, and her smile! But that group ended with me wondering, 'Did we make any difference with her, Jesus? Were you able to reach down deeper than we could see?"

Ashlie finished high school and college. I would see her often at church, exchange text messages, and loved giving her hugs. But I always wondered. Until …. Until I found her on Facebook. Until I began to read what she WROTE! And then I saw it. Under the quiet personality and the shy sweetness, Ashlie communicated by WRITING! And what she began to write revealed a depth of spirit, a depth of relationship with Jesus, a depth of understanding that I would never had known. Praise God for those who WRITE! For God's gift of communicating through the WRITTEN word. Ashlie had a gift.

And today? Ashlie has joined a small group of young adults at church. She is faithful with a capital F. She is so passionate about Jesus and people finding 'connection' that whenever visitors come on a Sunday morning, she immediately introduces herself and invites them to come join their group. She has a heart for those who need to be reached out to… those who need someone to ask them some questions, take time to listen, and invite them no matter what.

For a season, Ashlie continued to write the most beautiful devotional-type facebook posts that reached hundreds of people. She testified week after week to the faithfulness of God in her life, how he has healed some hurts, and given her courage. How He has loved her into wholeness and been faithful when she was lonely. Ashlie is like a ripple effect upon those who thought no one else could understand them. Ashlie boldly tells them she and Jesus truly do!

In Ashlie's Words

"One of the things I learned about God and his love for me through mentoring (versus just a book or podcast or class) is how much he values relationships and friendships in our lives. I've learned just how important it is to have Godly people in our lives who spur us on and cheer us on through every season, to help us grow and stretch our capacity to receive all He has for us.

One of the things my mentor taught me and passed along to me was a love for the Word. I still remember vividly the days she would text me a Bible verse and how much it encouraged me and reminded me to keep my eyes fixed on Jesus.

I really believe in Mentoring and discipleship. It's a gift to have someone come alongside you and pour into you and cheer you on to become all you were meant to be in Christ. It also has lasting impact for generations to come. It really has changed my life."

"To the fatherless he is a father. To the widow he is a champion friend. To the lonely he makes them part of a family."
Psalms 68: 5-6 TPT

Going Deeper

1. Think of a time in your life when you were new to a group or felt out of place in a certain environment. Was there someone who sought you out, asked you questions, and really listened? How did they 'invite you' into deeper community in the group? (And have you ever told them how much you appreciated them during that time?)

   _____

   _____

2. Is there anyone in your life who is incredibly shy or quiet? Have you at times thought they were uninterested or even unfriendly? Make a list.

   _____

   _____

3. Ask God for opportunities to get to know this person. How can you push past the outward facial expressions and begin to ask specific questions, take time to listen, and learn more about them? Remember, we cannot judge a book by its' cover nor a heart by its' facial expression!

   _____

   _____

CHAPTER 6

READY TO MENTOR
Tara's Story

"Mentors sacrifice their time and energy to be there for those they mentor. It can take them from their own family, marriage, and personal time. It's a sacrificial love unto the Lord to minister to others. It's a demonstration of the free gift of love that He offers."
-Tara

I believe Jesus has chosen you. He has called you! I believe he was speaking to ALL of his disciples when he said, "GO, and make disciples of all nations, baptizing them ...and teaching them to obey all I have taught you!"

I believe we are all called to make disciples, and do it the way Jesus did it: through mentoring relationships. But I also believe it's good to go in with our eyes wide open and have clear expectations: What does it take to be a mentor? What will it require from you?

In this chapter we will list some of these. Let's start again at the beginning with number one:

LOVE FOR JESUS:

Before making any disciples, I must first BE a disciple of Jesus who loves him with all my heart, soul, and mind. I must first say YES to His calling and know that I am doing this for and WITH the King that I love, by the power of His life within me!

TIME:

On the one hand, one of the benefits of mentoring in relationship is that you, the mentor, are not held to a church's schedule of programing, but can determine when and how often you meet, depending on your own schedule and that of your mentee's! There is flexibility! For example, during one season, I met with some girls BEFORE their school day so that I didn't fill up another night of the week. For other seasons and groups, we've needed a consistent night of the week, so it's every Thursday at 7:00 p.m., come rain or come shine for 8 weeks! Before beginning any of these, my husband and I look at the season we are in and determine what we have capacity for and what we do not. It's a team decision!

On the OTHER hand, TIME is one thing we will need to be willing to sacrificially and joyfully give! The older I get, the more it truly is one of my most precious commodities, but in this day and age of social MEDIA, time we can give to people IN PERSON may be the most important gift we can give. It may be the most transformative piece in mentoring: ***to give of our very lives is to love as Jesus did***.

Time is not just showing up, as you know. It is INTENTIONAL, and the more prayer I can give to my mentees IN ADVANCE, and throughout the week, the more it will knit my heart to both theirs and God's heart... so that when we DO come together, my heart is ready to impart what God has given me for them. ie. It takes preparation/prayer!

Time also needs to be joyful and CONSISTENT. THIS may be one of thee most challenging aspects of mentoring, but also the most needed! The most fruitful mentoring I've experienced has come from simple consistency. Even if it's only for a season, to be faithful and keep our word and our commitment is to model the faithfulness and value God has for them! Again, in today's world, this can be counter-cultural. To commit and keep the commitment is to be like God and to be a blessing to those who may have never experienced this in relationship! Building TRUST happens right here.

Probably one of the most DIFFICULT challenges of Mentoring is sticking with it when schedules get busy and your mentee cancels, and then cancels again the next week. Just this week I wrestled again with this one, "Should I just give up on this one? Or are you asking me to continue to pursue, Father?" I must be willing to be gracious, not resentful, and give them both the space to cancel AND an invitation to try again next week. When they see that you aren't going to bail easily, it encourages them to come; and coming encourages them to come again, for God's Spirit draws them always if we remain in His loving kindness! (This is another reason mentoring in groups can be so helpful: positive peer pressure draws them to be part of what's happening and looks forward to being together!)

A LISTENING EAR

This may seem obvious, but it can actually be hard to remember! If you are ready to mentor, then you probably have things that you are excited to share, advice to give, and wisdom to impart! But if we start with what WE have to share without first listening to where they are, we may miss what God is doing in the moment!

First, remember that people are starving for relationship. Even if they are surrounded by people, it's likely there are few people in their life, if any, that take time to sit, to ask questions, to listen, and to ask more. We were created by our relational Father to be KNOWN and heard, for this is the beginning of loving! Sometimes the greatest gift we can give is just space for another to share what's on their mind, on their heart, and what they're going through at this time. These are moments we create a safe space where they can just process, without always jumping in to solve anything or give any advice at all. This is where we hear what's going on deeper, and where the layers begin to be peeled back so we can know them more. These are the times to be praying, *"Holy Spirit, help me hear what's at the root of what they are saying; help me hear what You are showing me and how You would like to proceed next."*

One last thought, time together is not a counseling session, and it's good to model what 'healthy sharing' looks like by sharing from your own life. It does NOT look like a laundry list of all the things that have gone wrong this week. It does not look like time to bash their spouse or slander someone in their lives because they are hurt. It DOES look like helping them to be self-aware enough to know what things to bring to the group, things that they know they are stuck in, lies they may believing, or true struggles for which they know they need God's help and truth. Give a safe space to listen, but also be ready to turn the conversation when needed *away* from self-pity *to* encouraging self-awareness and what God is revealing!

VULNERABILITY

"If we claim that we share life with him, but keep walking in the realm of darkness (ie. where we hide from God & others, unseen and unknown), we're fooling ourselves and not living the truth. But if we keep living in the pure light that surrounds him (allowing God and others to see and know us as we are), we share unbroken fellowship with one another, and the blood of Jesus, His Son, continually cleanses us from all sin." 1 John 1: 8

Mentoring is not only about sharing the wisdom we have gleaned. It's also about sharing the struggles that we have been through or are currently going through, so that we model how we, too, rely on the help of Jesus and Holy Spirit in OUR times of need. This doesn't mean I share every dark thing I've ever done with every person I mentor; it does mean being real, being honest, and being open to what Holy Spirit wants me to share from my own life. The worst disservice we could do would be to only share our strengths. We must also be willing to share how we have failed at times, where we have missed it, and how we have received the grace and mercy of Jesus for our own lives.

Often, the greatest breakthroughs happen when we can help others remember that ALL of us need a Savior, and that the ground is quite level at the foot of the cross. The enemy loves to use SHAME to keep us from sharing the darker parts of our stories, for he whispers that we will not be loved or that we will be seen differently if we open up about 'that.' But those things we keep hidden are the very places we are stuck, and Jesus has come to set us FREE from that shame and guilt. The good news of the gospel is that Jesus already knows us and loves us just the same, and He wants us to experience that love through the unconditional love of his people. The Accuser wants people to think they are the only ones who struggle with 'that': The Spirit of Truth says you are not alone. Bringing it into the light exposes the lies that keep you isolated, reminding you how loved you are!

Steve & I have been doing Pre-marital mentoring for over 25 years. It's one of our FAVORITE types of mentoring. We have learned much and gleaned some wisdom from our 32 years of marriage, but honestly some of the most effective ways we have encouraged young couples is by sharing about the argument we had on the way to meeting with them! We need to keep it real! We share with them our struggles as well as our victories, and we share how we process through things with our good Father who alone softens our hearts, convicts us of sin, and restores us to right relationship. Be vulnerable with your stories. Give God the glory always. But let people see what it looks like to depend on our Savior in the messes of everyday life! This is equipping and discipling!

FAITH & PERSEVERENCE

Jesus said, *"I have come that you may have life abundantly!" "I have loved you as the Father has loved me! I have chosen you to go and bear fruit!" John 10:10, 15: 9, 15*

Jesus believes in you! You can do this! And Jesus believes in each one you mentor! Father created each one in His image to be LIKE HIM as a dearly loved child of God!

"But you are God's MASTERPIECE. He has created us anew in Christ Jesus, so we can do the good things he planned for us long ago!" Ephesians 2:10

Therefore, as His representative as a mentor, the greatest thing we can do is continually BELIEVE in each one and REMIND them of how amazing they are as God's masterpiece! There will be many days when they will not believe in themselves, they will hear only discouragement out in the world, and they will forget that they are a new creation in Christ! We need each other to REMIND each other of the truth! Experts say we are always 'talking to ourselves' and that the vast percentage of our self-talk is negative! It's also well known that it takes ten positive comments to override one negative comment we receive.

There will be days when no amount of talking or persuading can convince your mentee that it's ok and God loves them and forgives them! But you can always remind them that you see them, you know who they are, and you BELIEVE in them no matter what! Even and especially when they have really messed up, acknowledge the sin, but LOVE the sinner and remind them that this is NOT who they ARE (shame); it's simply something wrong they DID (healthy conviction). Remind them that this is precisely why Jesus died, that we can be forgiven and cleansed and made whole again!! It's good to cry with them, to take it seriously, and to even grieve for a season. But, point their eyes back to Jesus & 1 John 1: 9.

You may feel like they are not listening. You will often feel like nothing is happening and you will wonder if you're even doing any good at all. These are the times we must believe that we are planting seeds, and it takes time for seeds to grow into fruitful trees! You may feel like you're even wasting your time, but do not grow weary in doing good! Don't give up! Keep loving, keep believing, and keep persevering. It takes time. Keep believing that Jesus can reach any heart, His truth can set them free, and nothing is too hard for Him! It's true!

SPEAK THE TRUTH IN LOVE

We touched on this in chapter three when we talked about holding up the Truth of God's word like a mirror so that THEY can see the truth about themselves in the light of the Truth that can set them free. But there may be times when your mentee does NOT see the truth clearly or that their lives are not in alignment with God's will for them. We've all been there. We know there are times we must speak the hard truth in love.

There's no easy way to do this, so here are some quick thoughts on what I've learned. One, ask Holy Spirit for HIS timing, and be sensitive to feeling His peace before rushing in and pointing out their sin! Second, PRAY for your mentee. Pray and ask GOD to speak to them, show them the truth, and be gracious to bring conviction! Often, God will speak the truth to them before you ever have to! Our prayers matter, friends. God hears and moves when we ask Him!

Third, when you know it's time to speak – especially if you have real concerns about decisions they are making that could have real ramifications - ask a LOT of questions. Like, *"Tell me about this. Have you prayed about it? What do you feel like God is saying to you about this? What does His word say? How do you see this playing out?"*

Often, this may be only the FIRST conversation, and again we must see it as planting seeds that only the Holy Spirit can water and soften in their hearts. ***Our goal is NOT to tell them what to do***, but to remind them to trust God's good heart enough to ask HIM what to do next. Lead them in listening prayer. *"What is God saying? Let's wait and listen. What do you hear? What next step is He asking you to take?"*

And, if they are not ready to repent or change the way they are thinking, do not despair. Tell them you are so honored that they would be honest with you and be willing to talk about it. Affirm again that you believe in them and that you know they hear God's voice! Be patient in these times. Often, they will come back to you soon, having worked it out with God on their own. This is our goal!

Last, don't shy away from calling sin, sin! Don't shy away from the tough passages in God's word. Don't fear that they will never come back or want to meet with you again. If we have established that we love them, believe in them, and are fighting for them in prayer, they will be back! To love is to tell the truth BECAUSE we want them to be free, not enslaved to sin or the brokenness it brings! Our good, good Father loves them and wants only the very BEST for their lives, and this is why we can trust Him. Again, I John 1:9 says, *"If we confess our sins, he is faithful and just to forgive us our sins and to cleanse us from all unrighteousness!"* THIS IS THE GOOD NEWS! But, we can only be forgiven from what we CONFESS, meaning we AGREE with God that this is not His best for us!

I try to live a LIFESTYLE of Repentance, daily living in the light and sensitive to any conviction Holy Spirit may bring! I share this freely with my mentees: that this has become the way to live FREE from shame and FREE from the enemy's schemes! When we notice it, we confess it. As we go, every day. We are grateful for Jesus' blood! (A great resource on this subject is Roy Hession's book, ***The Calvary Road***)

TARA'S STORY

"I have had several mentors. It seems like I have been given a different spiritual mother/mentor at each stage of my adult life. There is something so powerful about a woman who has already walked through it and can understand, encourage, and listen. It is priceless. I'm so thankful that at each age and stage I have had the privilege to seek wise, Godly counsel. It's been life changing and has helped me immensely to stay the course and follow after Jesus.

Now that I mentor others as well, I understand what a precious gift it is when someone takes time to mentor me. It's real life. It's a relationship, not just knowledge that you read or learn about. It's truly experiencing Jesus with skin on!

One young lady I mentored several years ago was going through some very difficult times. Towards the end, she was beginning to reject some of the tough things I was communicating. In the end, she abruptly ended the mentorship, left the church, and abandoned all relationships in our circle. It was very painful. I had grown to love her so much. I knew that our hurts, wounds and sin can cause us to reject sound counsel, so I understood why. It still hurt.

Jesus is so good! He brought her back into my life 6 months ago! She came asking for forgiveness, and we are back in right relationship again. Of course, I forgave her in an instant with open arms and unconditional love... maybe the first time she had ever experienced unconditional love. He has restored our relationship! I am walking with her again through tough life circumstances, but this time she knows I love her and everything I have to say is built on a foundation of Christ's love."

GOING DEEPER

1. Of all the things listed above that mentoring will require from you, which do you have the hardest time applying? Ask God for HIS grace to empower you in this!

   _____

   _____

   _____

   _____

2. What does 'unconditional' mean to you? How is God asking you to apply it to a friendship, spouse, or mentoring relationship in your life?

   _____

   _____

   _____

3. Pay close attention to bitterness and resentment... if you find yourself feeling either one towards someone, stop and ask God why. Sometimes we must surrender again our own time and lives and remind ourselves we are giving these to Jesus for the ones He loves and died for.

4. Last, ask God to give you JOY in sacrificing your time and heart! Do things with your mentee that bring **you** life and joy as well ... and have FUN together. This is part of a real relationship, and models how Jesus loves spending time with us!

CHAPTER 7

READY TO BE MENTORED

Moms' Group Story

"I don't think I can overstate the value Mentoring has had in my life. Having someone/people who are for you and speak into your life on your behalf has, without a doubt, changed my life. I would not be who I am without these people." - Lindsey

Just as BEING a mentor will require some things from you, so does being MENTORED! Because this is a Relationship, it is a two-way street. Both parties must bring certain things to the table; both are needed to make this work well!

Many of the characteristics needed to be a great Mentee are the same as being a Mentor:

1. Are you ready to surrender your life completely to this wonderful Jesus and follow Him with all your heart as a true Disciple?

2. Do you believe in this enough, that Jesus has called you to learn and be His disciple, that you are willing and excited to INVEST TIME into this relationship? (Even when it's not convenient?)

3. Do you come with a humble and hungry heart, ready to LISTEN and learn from your mentor, God's Word, and His Holy Spirit?

4. Are you willing to be real, to be transparent, and be VULNERABLE

with your life, the good, the bad, and the ugly? There is great joy in learning to share honestly and freely … your mentor and Jesus love you so!

5. And are you open to your mentor, or others you trust in the group, speaking truth to you in love, even if it's hard to hear? Are you ready to invite them to speak into your life from God's word and His heart?

If so, God is going to bless you abundantly! In addition to these, there are also a few things that you as a Mentee can bring to this relationship that may surprise you!

For example, this is a wonderful time to learn to **INITIATE**!

Sometimes, someone may approach you and invite you into a mentoring relationship! But SOMETIMES, you may need to find the courage to ASK! First, ask God whom He might have in mind, and pray about the ones He highlights. Second, ask for some time or a coffee date that you could just ask some questions of a few of these people you know. It is so honoring to just want to know about someone's life and story with Jesus, to ask them questions about their own journey, and learn more about them. This can also be a time where YOU can discern whether this might be a good fit for YOU; does this person carry something you really want to grow in? Do you sense God's Spirit of love and kindness and truth upon them? Is there a connection?

You don't have to make any quick decisions; you can spend some time with them, then ask God in prayer if He's leading you to take the next step!

And if you feel a peace and excitement about it, go for it! Ask if they would be willing in this season to Mentor you! I know this is risky! It takes some courage, because the truth is, this person may NOT be able to mentor you during this time! But it's still a WIN for you: you did it! You obeyed what God was asking you to do! You are asking, seeking, and knocking as He encourages us to do in the Kingdom! Also, even though this may not be the right TIME, it may become the right time later, and you have planted a seed that may work out better down the road! You never know! And last, you have honored that person in the kingdom by asking them. God is a big believer in honoring each other; He himself honors us every day and is so pleased when His children do the same!

Initiation doesn't stop after the initial ask! In fact, when you DO enter into a mentoring relationship, you will want to continue to remember to ASK for what you are needing! Yes, you trust God to lead your mentor in how best to lead your time, your training, your curriculum. But there will be times when you know you need to get some good wisdom on something, or you know you are struggling in a certain area and need some direction... These are the times you get to SPEAK UP and let them know what's going on TODAY. Sometimes we wait and wish for people to 'notice' that we are in need, we want them to ask us and draw out 'what's wrong'; but a healthy relationship consists of two people who are straightforward and clearly communicate what they are needing, rather than hinting or acting differently in hopes that the other will ask. Just as we tell pre-marital couples, so it is with ALL relationships: *the other person cannot read your mind!!* It doesn't mean they don't care; it means you are responsible for speaking up and communicating clearly!

Last, don't hesitate to ask if there are SPECIFIC areas you want to learn about or be discipled in. For example, there are some people I want to learn about prayer from because they are PRAYER WARRIORS and they seem to pray God's heart in power! There are others I have asked to teach me how they 'hear' from God because I can see that they have a prophetic gift on their lives. What gets you excited when you talk about it? What do you wish you understood more? What books do you wish you had time to read? These could be topics you want to go after, and therefore people you want to ask, because this is what HOLY SPIRIT is saying and teaching YOU, and He's giving you a desire to pursue it!

MOMS' GROUP

During one season of my life, I was trying to meet with a number of different women individually. I found myself wishing I had more hours in the week to do this. Also at this time, a beautiful young newlywed named Kylea approached me, and INITIATED! She did the ask, and she did it well! She expressed to me how she knew she needed some wisdom and support during this new season of marriage. She knew there were others who felt the same. She was not only bold, she encouraged me that this was worth it! Then I felt the Holy Spirit give me the idea to invite them all into a group to do mentoring TOGETHER! I realized this particular group of women were all in similar stages of life: they were young marrieds with young kids. I also realized that one of my passions in life is seeing healthy marriages thrive and seeing parents equipped to raise their beautiful children in God's ways, in a world where neither of these is easy these days! Our boys were in high school and college and I felt a compassion for these young moms, for I knew what they were facing and how challenging it can be if you are trying to do life alone at this stage. I believe it still: we were not designed to do life alone! We were designed to do life together!

About this time, I was reading Titus 2:4 and saw this, *"These older women must train the younger women to love their husbands and their children, to live wisely and be pure, how to work in their homes, to do good, ..."* And it hit me for the first time: good heavens, that's ME! I'M now the Older Woman!

When I got over the shock of this new realization, I decided to embrace it and go with it! I said yes to Kylea and sent out invitations to 6 other amazing young moms whom I hoped would say yes. I realized three things as I made this list:

1. All of these young moms were also amazing LEADERS and INFLUENCERS, and I knew God had put each of them on my heart to encourage each of their own gifts and leadership in the

Kingdom. I knew they were raising mighty warriors for God. And, I knew their lives would create additional ripples of heaven wherever they went!

2. I really wanted to be intentional about committing to MENTOR these young moms in a deep and personal way. In RELATIONSHIP. Therefore, even though there were a LOT of young moms in our churches and neighborhoods, I felt Holy Spirit call me to keep this one a 'closed' group; not to be 'exclusive', but to be intentional about building relationship. When others heard there was a Mom's group, many were interested in coming. I felt a real peace and permission to explain this was a MENTORING group, and tried to help other moms find great groups like MOPS or prayer groups they could join. I share this because having clear goals helps us have clear boundaries, and that is ok in the kingdom! Jesus had CROWDS that he taught, and 72 that he trained and sent out at one time; but he only chose 12 to be his closest companions, to really pour into them, AND DO LIFE WITH THEM. None of us can be in deep relationship with much more than this! It's just a fact!

3. This would have to be Spirit-inspired and Spirit-led, because these women did NOT KNOW each other much at all, and each of these girls were very, very different in personality, giftings, and backgrounds! This was either going to work, or NOT!

Eight years have passed since that initial invitation. Many more babies have been born! (like 9-10 MORE). These amazing women not only said Yes to me, they said Yes to each other, and I have learned more from these girls than I could ever tell you.

We've studied the bible, learned more about marriage, read Parenting books and discussed them all, ... and learned to love deeply. They have cried & prayed and walked with one mom through a terrifying season of cancer treatments when her five-year-old was diagnosed. They've rejoiced together when a year later that same precious boy became cancer free! They've taken each other's kids in the middle of the night when one marriage crashed and burned and we all called on God for a miracle. They raised their hands and cheered when, a year later, this woman testified to the goodness of God saving her marriage!

They fight for each other daily; who knew group texts could unite us the way they do? They send scripture and prayer requests and meme's that make us laugh and no one else would understand! As I'm typing this, text messages are flying on subjects as vast as one praying for a grieving sister and another getting a stray cat out of her tree!

They have modeled for me Acts 2 and Acts 4 as they stay committed to meeting, to sacrificing their time, to love one another as Jesus has loved them. They have taught me to pray and declare the will of God and the heart of God and see answers within the day. We have story after story of marriage conflicts reconciled, fears about their kids relieved, and lies from the enemy taken captive and defeated in the name of our Jesus.

Sara has trained us all in healing prayer, and how to minister to each other by listening to God's voice. Charis has inspired us to be deep in God's word daily as it is our sword and answer for anything that comes. Lindsey has modeled a new way to do Sabbath with her family, encouraging us all to simplify and slow down and prioritize the precious gifts God has given us. Michelle sends out powerful worship songs on a regular basis, reminding us that Father inhabits the praises of His people and is so worthy of our praise! And as Amy begins to speak, she cries, as she feels the heart of God for you when no one else understands.

These girls represent the Body of Christ, each with a different gift and calling to build up the body and equip us to be God's disciples. This is God's 'church', His Ekklesia on the earth. His supportive, protective, and governing body bringing the kingdom and will of God here onto the earth as it is in heaven! And even as I write these words, I'm reminded that the reason I even STARTED thinking about writing a book on MENTORING Relationships is because Charis had a dream that I did, including the title and subject, the same week our son prophetically asked if I'd write such a book!

God speaks through His people. He calls us to *"encourage one another and build each other up."* When we started, we all went to the same church. Today, we go to four different ones! Seasons change but relationships remain, and even when Covid came, these girls have not stopped "the habit of meeting together." I pray I have passed on a few nuggets of wisdom as I have mentored these amazing women these past 8+ years; but as God would have it in His wonderful upside- down Kingdom, I have received even more from them. We have become family, and each of them has a place in my heart like no other, true spiritual daughters that THIS "older woman" is so blessed to call friends.

IN LINDSEY'S WORDS

"This group has brought so many things to my life; fun, accountability, wisdom, perspective, comfort, prayer, encouragement, vision, truth about who I am and what they see in me... SO MANY THINGS!

I was having a moment one evening. You know, one of those 'moments' that had lasted a little too long. I could tell my thoughts were not in a healthy place, and while I wasn't wanting to partner with the lies swirling in my head, I knew I needed someone else. I needed help. So, I called my mentor, a woman who has faithfully walked with me for years, knows the good, the bad, and the ugly. Someone I knew would speak truth in my life, but loved me all the same. I asked her if she could just come and pray for me. She came. And as we sat on my couch I began to just share the struggle in my heart, the hurt I was carrying, and that even though I knew the truth in my head, I wasn't able to get it to my heart. She listened, spoke truth, and prayed over me. It was what I needed in that moment to help me make the transition from head to heart. These are the moments that we all have in life... we all need someone/people who are helping us walk out this journey of life with Jesus. He designed us for it, and it is one of the sweetest, most beautiful gifts. I treasure it deeply.

I would say that BEING mentored requires initiation, humility, vulnerability, and trust. Ultimately, I am responsible for my walk with Jesus and my emotional needs. It is not the responsibility of my mentor to meet or anticipate every need I might have. I must ASK for help when I need it, be honest about what I am needing, and willing to listen and receive constructive feedback, trusting their heart is for me.

Being mentored also requires me to commit and invest. And the biggest commitment I have to give is my time. It does require our presence and consistency. The best relationships are those that have lasted many years. Most of the mentor relationships in my life flow from friendship, so it is more of a by-product of surrounding myself with people who love Jesus and me!"

"One of the areas in life that I am super passionate about is marriage. My husband and I love to mentor young couples who are engaged, sharing with them some of the things we have learned in our marriage, God's design for marriage, and try to help them navigate some of the questions they have before getting married. This is one of our greatest joys!"

And the Ripples of Heaven continue. . .

GOING DEEPER

1. Is there an older person in your life whom you truly admire and look up to? Have you seen good 'fruit' and results from their life of faithfulness in work, family, marriage, faith?

   _____

   _____

2. Pray and ask God if now would be a good time to ask this person to spend some time with you, even just for lunch or coffee. Put together some questions that you'd love to know about them that would honor them.

   _____

   _____

   _____

3. If there is connection, ask them to mentor you for a season. If this is not possible, ask if you could get together every now and then and continue to learn from them?

   _____

   _____

4. Are there friends or acquaintances around you that might also be looking for community/family/ a group to belong to? You may or may not be the most outgoing, but you may have eyes to see which people could use some connecting! Maybe start with a once a month thing. See how it goes. Ask God for HIS thoughts on all of this, and take time to listen. He is the best Gatherer and Father for his kids!

   _____

   _____

CHAPTER 8

SEEING THE ONE
Bailey's Story

"I felt seen and that someone believed in me... the one-on-one time with this mentor was invaluable to me. I had someone who was speaking life, joy, and truth to me. She would ask the tough questions, lead me through prayers, and allow room for the Holy Spirit to do what only He can do." - Bailey

The Power of One

I am a dreamer, a big-picture thinker! I have a strong desire for Jesus to be known throughout the whole earth! "Your name and Your renown are the desires of my heart, O God!" I literally want to change the world.

But I have learned that the best way to change the world is actually one life at a time, starting with the one or ones in front of me! Mother Teresa seemed to understand this better than anyone. She spent her life ministering to one leper after another in places in Calcutta that no one else would even dare to enter. She continually talked about how she saw Jesus in each ONE, and so she ministered to and served Jesus in each and every dying person she cared for. She wasn't in it for the accolades or fame or even a thank you. She served the ones who could do nothing for her in return. In my big-picture, big-impact personality, I have found I need to read and learn from this woman who knew the ways of Jesus so well.

> *"I alone cannot change the world,*
> *but I can cast a stone across the waters to create many ripples."*
> *"If you can't feed a hundred people, feed just one."*
> *"Be faithful in small things because*
> *it is in them that your strength lies."*
> *"It is not how much we do, but how much love we put*
> *into what we do. If you want to change the whole world,*
> *go home and love your family."*
> – Mother Teresa

Jesus said it this way, *"The King will reply, 'Truly I tell you, whatever you did for one of the least of these brothers and sisters of mine, you did for me.'" Matthew 25:40*

Then He told this story to let us know how important each ONE is to Him and His Father:

"If a man has a hundred sheep and one of them gets lost, what will he do? Won't he leave the ninety-nine others in the wilderness and go to search for the one that is lost until he finds it? And when he has found it, he will joyfully carry it home on his shoulders. When he arrives, he will call together his friends and neighbors, saying, 'Rejoice with me because I have found my lost sheep.' In the same way, there is more joy in heaven over one lost sinner who repents and returns to God than over ninety-nine others who are righteous and haven't strayed away!" – Luke 15: 4-7

Over many years of mentoring, there have been so many moments when I have thought, "Is this really worth it? Is it making any difference in their life?" And, honestly, I've had thoughts like, "I moved my schedule around 3 times and have sacrificed … to be here. Is anything really happening? Jesus, is this how you want me to spend these hours?"

It is. It is worth it. Over the years, I can now look back and see every hour given and every seed sown and tell you, it matters. Many times my weary body has just wanted to stay home and my skeptical heart has wanted to cancel. But I can honestly tell you I don't regret one moment of the times I pushed through, met with my "one", and simply asked, "How are you doing this week?"

You may wonder the same. You may need some encouragement today to say, 'Keep Going! Don't cancel! Persevere in love!" We all need the reminders. Jesus would leave 99 to go after the one. The one matters. The one no one will ever know you met with. The one who seems like they aren't really listening or possibly don't care about what you're saying. That one. Each one. Matters.

And what you will continue to read in these pages is that, more often than not, each ONE eventually turns around and affects the life of another ONE, who in turn, passes it on to another ONE. It only takes one stone thrown in the water to create ripples that cover the whole earth.

The Power of Chosen

My husband is not only a great leader, He has the spiritual GIFT of Leadership. He sees the one. He sees the potential in each one and calls them up higher to try things they never thought they could do. In both business and personal life, he takes time to say, "I see this in you. I'd like you to be on my team. I know you can do this."

The power of being seen and chosen changes people. Great leaders pull out the greatness in others. We, as God's representatives, are called to call out those who don't know they are called! We are to look for the gold that God has put in each one, and invite them to step into their 'calling.' First, they need to know God is calling them to be HIS! That He created them and has CHOSEN them to be His own, to be part of His family.

"Even before he made the world, God loved us and CHOSE us in Christ to be holy and without fault in his eyes. God decided in advance to adopt us into his own family by bringing us to himself through Jesus Christ. This is what he wanted to do and it gave him great pleasure!" Ephesians 1: 4-5

After receiving His calling to BE His child, we can THEN respond to the calling to DO...

"For we are God's masterpiece. He has created us anew in Christ Jesus, so we can do the good things he planned for us long ago." Ephesians 2: 10

And when you and I, as Mentors, can see the potential in someone, see the hunger, see the masterpiece underneath the scratches and the dents and the brokenness, we can help uncover the original design God planned for each one to be! This is what CHOOSING does.

"Hey, I know we don't know each other really well, but I wondered if you'd like to get coffee some time? I'd love to get to know you better!" "God brought you to my mind. Could we meet and chat some?" "I can see that God is pursuing you and speaking to you. Any interest in getting together to learn more about that?" "You have such a heart for prayer. I would love to gather and pray with you and maybe study prayer a bit. Would you join me?" "I'm looking for leaders to train up. I see "this" in you. Would you like to join us?"

God sees each one. He'd leave 99 to find one that was lost. He calls us to do the same!

Bailey's Story

"Being mentored has made all the difference in my life. I didn't grow up with much confidence in myself and would do anything to stay out of the way in most social situations. It wasn't until high school, when I started attending a new youth group that my perspective changed. Youth leaders were calling me up and asking me to contribute ideas, share what God was speaking to me, and participate in all that was going on! I felt seen and believed in! I was then invited to meet with one of these leaders and train to become a small group leader myself. The one-on-one time with this mentor was invaluable to me. I had someone (other than a parent) who was speaking life, joy, and truth to me. She would ask the tough questions, lead me through prayers, and allow room for the Holy Spirit to do what only He can do. Through mentoring relationships I started to understand the Father's heart towards me – He created me to carry the confidence of a beloved daughter and to lead others around me into the same revelation.

Experience can't be taught in a class, book, or podcast. Mentoring relationships have provided examples of what a lifestyle of Christianity can look like. Mentors have shown me what's possible and how to get there – just by sharing normal pieces of their life with me.

Over the past years, I've learned that my mentoring experience was unique and special. I can't expect that every mentoring relationship I make myself available for will go the same way as when I first experienced it. Every relationship is unique and will include different dynamics. In this season of life, I have established mentoring relationships with 3 girls younger than me – all of whom I meet with on a semi-regular basis and am available to call/text/talk when things come up! Even though we may not meet as a structured group right now, they see me every week and we spend time talking about the highs and lows. Just this morning I met with one of my girls before work and she opened up about how her thought-life was tormenting her with guilt and shame. We invited the Holy Spirit to lead the way. I had her ask Jesus some questions, and we waited on Him for the answers. She immediately heard His voice, and we left our time together with divine healing and strategy for the situation!"

GOING DEEPER

1. Is there someone in your sphere of influence who stays back in the shadows, doesn't usually say much, and lacks the confidence to step out? What has God put in them? Ask Him! What can you encourage them with or invite them to be part of? How can you help them feel chosen and seen?

   _____

   _____

2. Can you think of an example of 'the Ripple Effect'? Has someone that you have 'influenced' gone on to influence someone else? Or are you part of a chain that began a few people back, where ONE person decided to disciple another in the ways of Jesus? How has that been passed down to you?

   _____

   _____

3. In prayer, ask Father if there is a Lost Sheep that no one even knows is lost or alone. Ask Him to show you … often it will be someone that completely surprises you. Sometimes it will be someone who SEEMS to be part of the crowd, happy and content, but underneath they feel completely LOST AND ALONE. Father knows. He wants to share His heart with you, and He is inviting you to join Him in going after this lost and lonely one. (Just begin

to ask this person questions. Let them share where they are. Spend some minutes and listen well. Ask more. God will lead you to that One.)

(Note: Bailey sees the one like no one I've ever met. It is beautiful, and so is she. I'm especially thankful our son saw her, chose her, and asked her to marry him, and I can now call her daughter-in-law.)

CHAPTER 9

THE GOAL

How do we know if discipleship is really happening?!

Sarah's Story

*"By this everyone will know that you are my disciples:
if you love one another." -Jesus, John 13: 34-35*

"Begin with the end in mind," says Steven Covey, author of the book *7 Habits of Highly Effective People.* So, before we go any further, let's stop and remember what all of this is about: what is the end goal of "discipleship?" How can we tell if those we are mentoring are growing as disciples of Jesus?

It's love.

Love is the end goal of discipleship.

God is love. Jesus is what our loving God looks like in action, in human form.

Therefore, to be a disciple of Jesus means that I am growing in love, looking more like Jesus every day.

And the question I must ask is, "Are those I am mentoring loving well, forgiving quickly, obeying His word, and becoming more like Jesus every day?" This must be our goal and our measuring stick. . . Is discipleship happening?

True Story: Loving When It's Hard

When I first started mentoring, it was so exciting! Not unlike parenting, when you have their attention and they are excited to learn, it is pure joy to teach and train and watch them grow! I just wasn't prepared for the fact that it wouldn't always be this way: turns out that those we mentor still make mistakes, may choose to *not* listen to God's word, and may reject both God's Spirit – and me. Now, I realized that to "love" them meant loving them right there, in the midst of rebellion and rejection, no matter what. In past *friendships*, I had 'let go' of some of these relationships; they just kind of went away. But as a mentor, I knew I had to learn how to press in, step into the mess, and actually model unconditional love.

Because the Trio has met so consistently for so many years, they have afforded me many opportunities to learn about love! One season, two of them got into a huge fight and would not speak to each other. At this point, meeting together with four of us, and two not speaking – was pointless! I tried talking them out of it, showing them scripture, and was about to give up. Their hearts were hard and not ready to forgive. I learned to stop talking, pray, meet individually with them, and listen to what had offended them. I learned to ask questions, encourage them to ask Father, and I stopped trying to convince or convict. I learned this was Holy Spirit's job, not mine. My job was to love.

So I assured them both separately that I loved them and that I wasn't going anywhere. When the Holy Spirit had had his time, their hearts were softened, so we met to 'talk it out.' Again, I was not trained in 'reconciliation' or conflict resolution, but I learned it on the job! It seemed good for them to have this conversation in the safety of our mentoring group; though hurt and unsure of the future, they were in a safe place where they were supported and could talk it out. We learned how to be honest and honoring at the same time. We learned how to own our own part of the conflict. We learned how to truly apologize for how we had hurt one another, and how to extend forgiveness even before we felt it. These conversations – on many occasions - were uncomfortable to say the least; they were crazy hard. It would have been 'easier' to just say I'm sorry and sweep the rest under the proverbial rug. But we learned that true reconciliation happens when we confess our sins to each other, are vulnerable about our hurts and hang-ups, and live in the light as He is in the light. These were the days when God's word was our only compass. To love one another as He loved us is not easy, but it is the way to freedom and depth of relationship. If Jesus could forgive us and extend grace when we didn't deserve it, He could empower us to do the same for each other.

In the Old Testament, the Israelites lived their entire lives by the Hebrew "Shema", stated clear back in Deuteronomy 6:5-6

"Hear, o Israel! The Lord is our God, the Lord alone. And you must love the Lord your God with all your heart, all your soul, and all your strength. Commit yourselves wholeheartedly to these commands....

When an expert in religious law came to Jesus and asked him what was the most important commandment, Jesus replied,

"You must love the Lord your God with all your heart, all your soul, and all your mind. This is the first and greatest commandment. A second is equally important: 'Love your neighbor as yourself.' The entire law and all the prophets are based on these two commandments." Matthew 22: 37-40

In other words, if we LOVE, first God and then each other, we will 'automatically' obey all his other commands!

On the night before he left the earth, Jesus took the age-old command and raised it. He added one more thing. He told his disciples what this LOVE *looked* like:

"So now I am giving you a new commandment: Love each other. Just as I have loved you, you should love each other. Your love for one another will prove to the world that you are my disciples."
-John 13: 34-35

And how has Jesus loved us? He laid down his life for his friends. Not because they deserved it, but specifically when they did NOT deserve it: when they had abandoned Him and denied they even knew Him, and one even betrayed Him to the authorities to be crucified. And there on the cross, abandoned by most who had followed Him and mocked by those killing Him, he said this, *"Father, forgive them, for they know not what they do."*

Today, we are 'making disciples' if we are modeling and training and inspiring others to forgive and lay down their lives for their friends or spouses, especially when their friends and spouses do not deserve it. And it will be evident to all who is growing into true disciples of Jesus: they will love one another as He has loved us!

Sarah's Story

In another season with the trio (remember, we've been meeting for over 16 years, from 7th grade on through college and dating and now marriage and babies…..) Sarah went off to college. Always the sweet one who saw the good in everyone, the three of us at home were praying she would also see and remember the good in herself. We quickly realized this was her time, she was going to have to find out who she was, who her God was, and what living loved by Him looked like in the real world where everyone worked hard to earn love.

Praise God she remained connected and did not pull away! Praise God she was honest and shared her struggles, her questions, and even some of the decisions she regretted. And praise God he was with her as she walked it out, and with us as we learned to love and believe in her and remind her who she was… no matter what. That season, we learned to pray. To intercede. To never give up.

During this time, I watched her two BFF's continue to support her, go visit her, get to know her 'new friends', and never pull away. I learned to listen MORE and ask more questions, and continually declare my own love for her. And it was sincere; we truly knew God's heart for her, and we believed in her and reminded her who she was in Jesus, even when she wasn't sure of it herself!

Sarah is a hero of mine. She not only made it through that time, she came through knowing who she was and how much her Father loved her! She met an amazing young man who also wanted to be an authentic disciple of Jesus, and the two of them came to Steve and me and asked us to do their pre-marital counseling = mentoring. They came with hungry and humble hearts, a true desire for a godly marriage, and a deep longing to become like Jesus in their relationship. The day they were married, I looked back and realized, 'God is so faithful. God loves us through our tough seasons. God never gives up on us.' And we cried tears of true joy and gratitude!

Today, Sarah & Luke are parents of two precious baby girls, serve faithfully in their church, and lead an amazing small group of …. you guessed it… *college students* who are figuring out who they are. They invite them into their home, walk with them through their struggles, and fight for them in prayer. They weep with them and celebrate with them and love them unconditionally, no matter what. They are mentoring and making disciples for the Jesus they love. Like two pebbles thrown in the water, their lives are now affecting other lives, who go on to influence other lives, like ripples from heaven.

In Sarah's Words

"Oh, how thankful I am for long time mentoring and consistent relationship! The benefit of mentoring for me specifically has been rich words of truth and advice from within the safe bounds of being known and loved relationally. I tried on quite a few "selves" in high school and college, trying to figure out who I was and who God wanted me to be. I found that those two questions were actually asking the same thing! Being able to come home from college not only to a nuclear family that loved and valued me – even when I wasn't acting very loveable -- but also to close friends and a mentor who I really looked up to… this became a safe space to 'hit the reset button.' I was known and loved not for what I did or didn't do, but simply for who I was.

God's love has been played out in real life! We did bible studies, listened to great teachers, and then celebrated birthdays with lunch outings and thoughtful gifts. I experienced God's love through my mentor as she modeled that I was worth celebrating. I learned that God rejoices over me with singing, he loves to give his kids good gifts, he is delighted with me! I felt that in 'real time' as my mentor carved out time for me to be celebrated, treated, valued, and honored.

Our bible study meetings eventually evolved into 'How are you doing? What's happening in your life?' I know there were times I didn't really open up, I was fearful, ashamed, unsure and didn't take hold of the love and resources made available to me. But my Trio & MLo stuck with me even then!

Today, my husband and I lead a small group at our church. We've had the great honor to see several college students be saved and turn around to tell others about who Jesus is and what he does. We've seen dozens learn more about their faith and what that looks like played out. Most of the students and young adults we've led and loved have been with us for a time and then moved away or gone to go disciple others.

But some relationships have stayed with us longer... and transitioned into mentorship!

One young lady came to our group from a wrecked family with manipulative parents and no knowledge of or experience with God. And though my situation had been different, I had a heart of love and long suffering for her because my mentor had had one for me. We were there when she accepted Jesus. I saw the look on her face the first time she heard the Holy Spirit speak and the first time she prayed with power. I cried with her when she confessed chronic sin she'd hidden for years and the sadness she had walked through. She even lived with us for a time. She loves us like family, and we know that being present in her life is such a gift, a privilege and an opportunity to give what we've been given. She needed someone to stick with her, and we will do that for as long as God says to do it!"

GOING DEEPER

1. Are there any relationships you have given up on, whether mentoring or just friendship? Ask Holy Spirit if there are ways you could press in and continue to love them?

   _____

   _____

2. Have you become discouraged when someone you mentored or discipled chose to go a different direction? Ask Jesus, "Have I felt offended or rejected? Do I need to forgive? Show me how YOU did it for those who rejected you." Write what you hear.

   _____

   _____

3. Sometimes we don't want to 'condone' someone's behavior, so we withhold our love and approval. (This is called 'religion'.) Ask God how HE does it! How does HE see them, believe in them, and love them where they are? How did He do it for you?

_____

_____

_____

CHAPTER 10

GOD'S PART & YOUR PART

WHO'S RESPONSIBLE FOR WHAT?

Monica's Story

"Remember your leaders who taught you the word of God.
Consider the outcome of their way of life and imitate their faith."
Hebrews 13:7

"When I think about my mentoring/discipleship relationships, I
am often deeply moved by how someone here on earth could care
so deeply about me, and yearn for me to grow and experience
God's love." -Monica

Thirty years. I've had the blessed privilege of discipling others through mentoring relationships for over thirty years now. I thank God for the great joys of getting to partner with Him in fulfilling Jesus' Great Commission to go and make disciples. And that is what it is: a Partnership, a Co-Mission where we are called Co-laborers with Christ! We are not called to mentor on our own, or make disciples on our own, for Jesus himself concludes his Commission with "And I will be with you always!!!" It's only BECAUSE He is with us that we can do this!

"Remain in me, and I will remain in you. For a branch cannot produce fruit if it is severed from the vine, and you cannot be fruitful unless you remain in me. Yes, I am the vine; you are the branches. Those who remain in me, and I in them, will produce much fruit. For apart from me you can do nothing." John 15: 4-5

Thank you, Jesus, for teaching us! A branch must be connected to the vine, it's source of Life, for any life to flow into and through the branch! And what is it that flows from the Vine to the Branch to bring it life? The SAP = the Holy Spirit = Jesus With Us! Only when you and I abide, live from, stay connected to, find our life source IN JESUS the Vine can we find the Life, the nourishment, the strength that we need to bear fruit! Only when we invite and allow Holy Spirit to flow from Jesus into us and abide in us and be our Source of all life and fulfillment will we ourselves thrive, blossom, and naturally overflow with fruit for others.

Our part in mentoring, our part in ALL of life, is to remain connected to Jesus by His Spirit. God's part is to bear His fruit through us!

There is no striving in the Kingdom! He truly is responsible for the outcomes; we are responsible to abide or 'stay connected' to Him like plugging into a source for more juice or more power! It's then that His Spirit of power flows right through us.

We are called to love, invite, listen, care, teach, model, mentor. But God himself, by His Spirit, is the only one who convicts of sin, transforms a heart, and makes people NEW by His Spirit in them!

All pressure is off!

> It is our job to hold up the mirror, the Word of God, so that the Spirit of God can speak to them: *"When he comes (the Advocate /Holy Spirit) he will convict the world of its sin, and of God's*

righteousness, and of the coming judgment... When the Spirit of Truth comes, he will guide you into all truth." John 16: 8, 13

➤ It's also our job to teach them to listen and hear and recognize God's voice when He is speaking to them. *"My sheep listen to my voice; I know them, and they follow me." John 10: 27*

➤ And finally, it's our job, not to give them our opinions or our advice, but to **remind** them of what God has already told them. Because they will forget. I do. You do. Every day. We need each other to remind us what is true, what God has said. And we need to be in RELATIONSHIP with each other enough and know each other's history enough to be able to REMIND them, "Remember when God spoke to you through that scripture? Remember how you knew it was Him?" or "Remember when you got that prophetic word about how God sees you, and that name HE has given you, and that song He is singing over you? Remember'"

Because it is the Holy Spirit's job to convict and transform, we all need to hear it straight from Him! It is His kindness that leads us to repentance; it is the power of His gospel that alone can save us!

So, if you're pouring into and investing in people, and your heart is breaking because they are going astray, or not living in the truth, remember. You cannot just 'change their mind' or tell them how to behave. Be filled with His Spirit, ask for His wisdom, love them well, and point to the Word of God. He alone will be the one to truly speak to and change a heart!

We are not responsible for the outcomes. We are not responsible for others' choices or decisions. We cannot change ANYONE. We leave these things for our good Father!

WE are called to love, to be available, to listen, to model, to pray, to ask questions, to lead them to the Word, and pray they be filled with His Spirit so they can hear His voice for themselves.

He will handle the rest.

Monica's Story

"If there's anything that you have taught me about a discipleship relationship, it is 1) to be real, 2) to be gracious, and 3) to bring it back to the gospel. You've shown me how our relationship with the Father applies in all scenarios of life and how real Christ is in our everyday. My meetings with you have only left me feeling fueled with encouragement and love, never guilt, shame, or brokenness. And I think that's what men and women need on their path towards growing in a relationship with Christ.

I have been in a mentoring relationship with a younger woman for almost a year now. We have been going through a book that is beneficial for her current season of life, but sometimes we just need to connect and chat. Being intentional about meeting with her can be difficult, but knowing the positive experiences I've had with being mentored in my life, it encourages me to prioritize my time with her.

I have learned that being raw with your mentee provides a sense of vulnerability that creates an open door for more transparency. For example, this young woman I am discipling has been afraid of sharing certain details of her life to me or how she has 'messed up.' I've been able to open up about mistakes in my past and present, and she feels so much more comfortable knowing that I have been there. This can mean that hard questions have to be asked, but most importantly she is getting a gracious response rather than a condemning one. I have been making an intentional point to show where the Spirit has moved in her life and how He is present. This has been life-changing for her. I'm thankful that even in the most mundane of conversations, you have taught me to bring it back to the reality of who God is and how we abide with the Father."

GOING DEEPER

Have you ever felt responsible for another person's walk with the Lord? Ever felt the pressure that you must be doing something wrong, or that you need to do more? Use the check list below to see if you have taken responsibility for things that only God can do:

Have you ever (check ones that apply)

___ spent hours worrying about them?

___ dropped everything each time this person called because 'they needed you?'

___ spent hours talking, only to feel that you are getting nowhere?

___ continued to deal with the same issues over and over again?

Today, confess where you have taken responsibility for things God never intended! Thank Him that He alone is responsible for the outcome of this person! Pray and release them to His care, know that they are in good hands, and let them go. Abide again, connect again to Jesus! Take a deep breath of His Spirit! There's no striving in the Kingdom! God's got this!

CHAPTER 11

STICKING WITH THE WAYWARD ONE

Heather's Story

"Love never gives up, never loses faith, is always hopeful, and endures through every circumstance." 1Corinthians 13: 7

It was a cold, damp, and foggy early morning, and I was trying to get my key to fit into the lock on the boiler room door of the church. This had become our weekly meeting place and time, each Friday at 7:00 am. These two girls had said Yes to my invitation to meet before school, and the only place we could find to meet that was close to their school was a little Friends Church on Main Street who graciously offered us the use of their boiler room! Looking back, it makes me laugh that we accepted! Add to that: we were studying the book of Revelation, with all its plagues and dragons and … there in that dark, dusty boiler room . . . But it was all part of the adventure!

Over thirty years have passed since then, but I will never forget those early mornings with Heather and Amanda in the boiler room! I had met these precious girls at our Campus Life meetings at their school; they would stay around after it was over and just chat, asking me questions and giggling a lot (as 7th and 8th graders do!). Eventually, I felt God nudge me to invite them into more: into bible study and time together outside of school. "We can study any book of the bible you want," I had said. *"Oooh! How about Revelation? I've always wanted to read it!"* "Well, that's probably not where I would start, but OK! Let's do it!"

And so began a relationship with two sweet girls whom I grew to love and thoroughly enjoy, even through the giggles, the non-stop talk about boys, and the cold early mornings! We eventually got to meet in better conditions, moving on to classrooms and eventually my house as they got older and could drive themselves!

What I didn't see coming, however, were the turns these girls' journeys would take after they graduated. Still new at this mentoring thing, I probably should have seen it, asked more hard questions, spoken more truth in love; but I was young as well, and I did not.

When Amanda told us she was getting married, we were excited, then asked the "And he's a Christian, right?" question. If memory serves me correctly, she answered that he had gone to church with her a few times and "was open?" They moved out of state soon after. I started having babies. We lost touch for a few years.

When Heather decided to move to another city with her boyfriend, I asked if we could meet. When she stopped calling or returning my calls, I knew I needed to pray. This is one of thee hardest parts about mentoring; or rather, about loving and caring: when they stop returning your calls. When they go silent. When you know that they have chosen to go their own way and they don't want to hear the truth they know you will speak. If you risk it to love and care, and certainly if you take the risk to mentor, this will happen. It is part of life. It is part of loving. It is part of allowing people to be free to make their own choices and have their own journey with Jesus without trying to control them. This is the way Father has loved us. This is what love does. And it can be painful. But it is worth it.

It Will Happen. What You Can Do

So, what do you do when you are worried about them, when you fear they are making poor choices, and when your heart is breaking for them? I confess I sincerely didn't KNOW what to do back then; but here are a few things I've learned over the past 30 years. **(Parents, take note: this is also applicable to those difficult years of 'discipling' your teens. I know this from experience, too.)**

➢ **Pray.** Pray consistently God's word over them each day. Take the worry and turn it into prayer. Pray prayers of FAITH over them; not prayers of pleading. Remember your Father loves them more than you do and knows where they are, and He wants you to *join Him in agreeing with Him in prayer concerning them!* Example: *"Thank you, Father, for this precious one! Thank you that You created them in your image, a unique masterpiece that you love so dearly! Thank you for the gifts and talents you've put in them! Thank you for the plans and purposes you have for their life! Thank you that nothing can thwart your good plans and purposes in the end! Today, I ask you to reveal Yourself to them in dreams, whispers, encounters! Remind them of Your great love for them! Remind them that you alone know them well and understand them! Remind them of all you have spoken to them in the past! Surround them with your angels, protect them from evil and the evil one! Silence the voice of the enemy in their ears, and enable them to hear your voice of love and direction over their lives! Soften any hard places in their hearts and immerse them again in Your Spirit's presence and love! Send Godly friends, voices and influences into their lives! Give them a distaste for anything that is not of you! Convict them with the truth in your kindness and love until they no longer desire the short-term pleasures that have come to enslave them. Give me scriptures to pray over them, Father! Thank you that you hear me. I entrust them into your loving care!"*

➤ **Speak Words of Life:** When you can speak to them or text them, remember that your words are powerful! Speak words of encouragement over them, to remind them of who they are and build them up; not tear them down. Every word of honor or respect you can speak will water the seeds of greatness that are lying dormant within, seeds that God put in them! Affirm your love for them! Tell them you believe in them, even if they aren't believing in themselves! Tell them you see and know the amazing man or woman of God they are created to be, and that you are always there for them, no matter what! Remind them that your love is not based on what they do, but who they are. Remind them to keep talking to their Father, to keep asking Him questions. Remind them that He alone is trustworthy and faithful, and will always tell them the truth!

> *"Do not let any unwholesome talk come out of your mouths, but only what is helpful for building others up according to their needs, that it may benefit those who listen." Ephesians 4:29*

➤ **Do not take it personally.** Don't take offense. This is not about you, but about their own journey with Jesus. They are having to form their own relationship with Him, not dependent on you or their parents or youth group or Pastor … they have to find that He is real for themselves. Remember that Jesus knows how you feel for He was abandoned, denied, and betrayed by His closest friends. Ask for His heart. You will feel angry, because it hurts to be rejected and ignored, and it feels you are not valued. But turn that anger towards the real enemy, and remember that greater is He that is in you than he that is in the world. You have the same power that raised Jesus from the dead living in you, and you have access to the courts of heaven where you can enter boldly to the throne of grace to ask for help in your time of need, to advocate for the one you love, and to make declarations and decrees as a member of God's church = His ruling and legislative body on the earth! It's time we step up and realize the authority He's given us in the spirit to forbid on earth what is forbidden in heaven, and to release in the earth what is already released in heaven. **As His child, you represent the King in all 'legal' matters in the spirit. Learn how to use the authority He's given you in the lives where you have divine influence!**

➤ **Last, Never Give Up!!** Oh, the joys of those who persevere!! This is how Jesus has loved us: he believes in us, trusts us to return, and died for us while we were still sinners! This is what love does. Love frees people to make their own choices; it gives them free-will. But it stands on the porch and watches for their return! And runs to meet them when they begin the long journey home! Love whisks them up in a big hug, forgives them before they ask, and re-instates them into the Family of unconditional love and acceptance! It helps them clean up their mess, confess their sins, and receive the cleansing forgiveness that only Jesus can bring! Love steadies them and walks alongside while they are re-learning to walk, breaking old habits, and making things right with both God and man. Love is patient. It is also kind. It rejoices when they take a step towards wholeness! It picks them back up if they stumble again. Love never gives up. It always believes, always trusts, always perseveres....

STORIES OF GRACE and Happy Endings!

It was years before I realized the painful journeys that Heather and Amanda had endured. I had no idea that one was suffering in a difficult marriage that eventually did not make it. Or, that while we were meeting in boiler rooms and giggling through the junior high years, one was enduing trauma and brokenness at home that was shaping a young girl's heart and mind. I had no idea. But God did. And He was there. He was with them.

And this God that we call Rescuer and Redeemer and Savior and Deliverer, was all these things and more to Heather and Amanda. He brought them through it, He has loved them towards wholeness, and He has been healing the deepest places along the way.

Today, I thank God for these girls, and for their stories of Grace. I thank Him that they are living testimonies of what our God can do with any heart that turns back and surrenders again. And, praise God, I thank Him that I can call Heather and Amanda my dear friends! I thank Him that they live close, are in my life, and that the three of us are even serving alongside each other in the Kingdom!! What a joy! What a God we serve!

Today, these amazing women are in Kingdom marriages, raising beautiful kids, and serving the world around them. Amanda is an amazing business and community leader in the area, and Heather serves as the Children's Director at our church! Both have an astounding gift of seeing the hurting, serving the broken, and extending grace to all who need it; for they themselves have received, and now they freely give.

In Heather's Words

"At my lowest, I seemed to always go back to her, this woman who came into my life when I was reeling from the pain of abuse and my misguided attempts at love. Never was there a moment I was told who I should be ... or an attempt to get me to change in order for me to be loved by her. But there was a passion in her that, even now, it resonates today; it still burns with a desire for me to be better. Not better to earn love, but better because I am loved.

Mentoring to me is like intimate teaching into someone's heart and soul. I've been given the freedom of knowing I can't out-sin God's love; that everything He says is true and his word is unwavering. From my mentors' examples, I learned God is faithful to keep his promise, and in those relationships, they would make me promises and KEEP them. I found that, for me, it was in the practical ways I saw and learned about God's love ... his kindness, his goodness towards me, and his unending love.

I got to mentor a college student a few years back, and she had lots of questions about God. She was like a sponge, and it was so neat to watch her heart open up to him. But about 6 months into dating a particular guy, things took a turn she had not planned on, and she confessed to me… Here it was. Here was my chance to show her the love I was given all those years ago. I loved her just as she was without the expectation that she would change, but all the while sharing the truth of God's loving ways. He is a gentle leader. God had broken through my own shame until I finally believed that His love came with no strings attached."

GOING DEEPER

1. Have you ever mentored, or invested in, someone who chose to go their own way and rejected the things you thought you both shared? How did this make you feel? How did you respond?

   _____

   _____

2. Is there currently someone that you are concerned about, knowing they are making poor choices? How can you be a voice of encouragement in their life? How can you be an extension of God's love that is not based on their behavior – with no strings attached? Ask God what steps He might have you take? Listen. Write what you hear!

_____

_____

_____

_____

3. Do you know it's time to speak some truth in love? Begin by asking them questions about the situation. Ask them how they see it playing out. Ask them if they've asked God about it. If they still need it, gently remind them that you love them and you want God's very best for them; you long for them to not be deceived by the enemy who tells us God is holding out on us. And show them the truth of God's word in the context of God's love for them.

_____

_____

4. Have you let shame from your own past keep you from thinking God could use you to mentor or disciple someone else? Can you see from the examples above that sometimes the very things God saved us from are the places we can help someone else who is struggling with the same? Ask God how He can use your own brokenness in His redeeming way to actually be a blessing of encouragement and healing and truth in someone else's life! Ask and listen.

_____

_____

_____

5. If you still feel you are 'disqualified', ask God what lies you are believing. (These usually sound like condemnation and shame, which come from the Accuser). Write what you hear. Then, come

into agreement with what GOD says is true and break agreement with any lies He reveals. Break these agreements out loud! (and symbolically scribble out what you wrote!) Last, ask God what His truth is INSTEAD.... Listen. Write what you hear! Then speak it over yourself. He is so proud to be your Abba!

_____

_____

_____

_____

_____

_____

_____

_____

_____

_____

_____

_____

_____

CHAPTER 12

A WATCHFUL EYE FOR UNHEALTHY TIES

"Every time I think of you, I give thanks to my God... And I am certain that God, who began the good work within you, will continue his work until it is finally finished on the day when Christ Jesus returns. So it is right that I should feel as I do about all of you, for you have a special place in my heart."
Philippians 1: 3, 6

Jesus is our purest example of discipling through mentoring relationships. But his disciples naturally continued this practice as THEY made disciples, so we can also learn from their examples as well.

The Apostle Paul, especially, always had someone WITH him, someone who was not only assisting him but learning from him. He speaks of Barnabas and Silas and "my son, Timothy." In the passage above, he refers to a group of people whom he had poured into and discipled and loved.

But Paul's examples also remind us that relationships are tricky; in fact, because relationships involve two imperfect people, **all** relationships are messy! Paul got frustrated with people, got his feelings hurt, and even parted ways with people! I think we can learn from THESE kinds of examples as much as from the ones that were loving well! Note his rebuke to the Corinthians:

> *"For some members of Chloe's household have told me about your quarrels, my dear brothers and sisters. Some of you are saying, 'I am a follower of Paul.' Others are saying, 'I follow Apollos,' or 'I follow Peter,' or 'I follow only Christ.' Has Christ been divided into factions? Was I, Paul, crucified for you?" I Cor.1: 11-13*

As with any good gifts that God sends, our temptation as human beings will always be to worship the gift over the Giver! The believers in Corinth were bragging or arguing about which 'person' had discipled them, instead of being united in the One Savior, Jesus, who alone had died for them!

In my thirty plus years of Discipleship RELATIONSHIPS, I -like Paul – have not always gotten it all right! There have been some conflicts, some hurt feelings, and – dare we say it – some unhealthy ties or dependencies! There have been times in my younger years when I unintentionally acted as my mentee's 'savior', always there for them, always available to have the right answers, and – let's be honest again – finding great pride in "all the ways I could help them." This was not only unhealthy for ME, but it created for them a dependency upon me that should have been directed and placed upon Jesus and His Spirit within them!

And, in a weird sort of way, we mentors also must fight the temptation to not become too dependent on those we mentor: sometimes we don't realize how much we have relied on their appreciation, their thanks, or their admiration. Sometimes, we are unaware of how we find our purpose, fulfillment, or even our identity in "being so & so's mentor!"

Over the years, I began to grow – thank you, Jesus – in my discernment and just plain maturity. I began to recognize when the healthy mentoring ties were becoming 'unhealthy,' and God has been faithful to keep teaching me over the years. He graciously uses past mistakes to not only teach us and prepare us for next relationships, he uses them to keep us humble and dependent upon Him!

When writing the outline for this book, I felt Holy Spirit remind me that this is one thing I wish I had known thirty years ago, before starting to mentor. So, I include this list below to hopefully equip you and possibly save you from having to learn the hard way!

Keeping A Watchful Eye for Unhealthy Ties in Mentoring

➤ Stop and ask yourself and God these questions, and then wait and see what He says to you in response. This can be uncomfortable, but OH, so freeing as Holy Spirit is always faithful to reveal anything that has taken the place of Jesus upon the throne of our hearts!

1. Whose opinion do you consider first before speaking or making a decision? (Sometimes, we mentors want to impress our disciples so much that we let 'fear of man' become more important than a healthy fear of what God thinks!)

2. Whom do you need to be OK with in order to function? (If a conflict with someone has derailed you or caused you to emotionally crash, these are red flags that reveal co-dependency. Look to the Father for His great love for you, and 'cut' that unhealthy tie in the spirit! -see below)

3. If you are being mentored, do your feelings get hurt when your mentor doesn't respond right away, or text you right back? Do you wonder if they are 'mad at you' or disappointed in you? Go to Father in prayer, and ask Him to remind you how secure you are in him, how to assume the best, and how not to place unrealistic expectations on ANYONE. If this has been an area of struggle for you, do not despair. Find a counselor or pastor or healing prayer

ministry like Sozo or Heartsync or C.R. But first, try the following: Holy Spirit is called 'The Counselor!' We have within us the most wonderful counselor who knows us best and loves us most and desires that we live free and healthy! Taking time to sit with Him and ask Him questions, and allowing Him to ask me some back, has been life changing for me! If you feel that any of the above applies to you, or has in the past, He is so proud of us when we come to Him for 'counseling!'

Here's a prayer you can pray, *"Father, what does this (anything you've learned from the above questions) reveal about my heart? Have I become too dependent on this person, or they upon me?"* (If you feel He is showing you YES, you can break these ties in the spirit, without having to 'break' or throw out the relationship completely!) *"Father, I agree with you that I have made _____ an idol and depended on them in ways I am to depend upon you alone. Please forgive me, and cleanse me. I renounce this dependency, and I cut this unhealthy tie from having any hold on me. I look to you, Jesus, as my only Savior and Lord, and the One who meets my needs and loves me completely! Thank you for setting me free from this unhealthy tie, and give me a healthy love for _____ with no strings attached! Is there any other truth You want to show me, Father? I humble myself before you and am listening for your kind heart:* "

_____

_____

_____

_____

_____

CHAPTER 13

TAKE THEM ALONG

Jasmine's Story

"Having a mentor feels like having a joyful cheerleader of faith in my life! I could never imagine NOT having a mentor. I mean, it's like trying to go the gym without knowing how to use the machines, so you rely on your own understanding… you need an accountability partner that runs with you, and does leg day with you, and encourages you to not give up…" - Jasmine

Hunger. That's what we saw in Jasmine when she got back from DELIGHT Ministry's Fall Retreat. She was not the same girl she had been a week before– she had truly encountered the extravagant, doesn't-make-sense love of God for her, and this girl was on fire!

Bailey and I laughed and cried and thanked God right along with her as she recounted her experience: how everyone came into the Light of God's love with authenticity and vulnerability, and confessed their sins, and let go of burdens, and received forgiveness … for things they thought they could never tell anyone. She had danced in the river, been washed by the blood, and could not stop praising the God who loved her so deeply.

It is fun to be around this kind of fire. It re-ignites the flames that can sometimes grow dim in each of us. It reminds us of the extraordinary magnificence of the Gospel of Jesus, and awakens us again to the awe and wonder of such a good Father! Hungry people are the most fun with which to share the Bread of Life!

So even though our second son was 'dating' this precious girl, I could not stop inviting her to things (and unofficially mentoring as we went). "Wanna go to a Worship Night?" was met with, "YES! Can we dance on the front row? Can we stay all night? Why do they have to be so short?" And so we went! We went to worship nights and conferences and any place we could be near the fire of God's presence and pour out our love on Him.

And there was no structure or set meeting times, but we would hang out on my porch for hours as she asked questions, inquired about the Bible, and shared the latest ways God had spoken to her and encountered her again!

It soon became evident to me that Jasmine had a prophetic gift; and it was so fun to help her discern that it was Holy Spirit who was speaking to her, showing her pictures in her mind's eye, and revealing truths in her dreams and in the scriptures that she had never seen before. And because she is a gatherer, it wasn't long before she invited a friend – or two – or three – and one of their moms – then their sister, or two…

As a mentor, I was pretty much in seventh heaven! What a privilege to be a part of someone's faith journey as you watch them grow into the amazing disciples, then witnesses, then leaders that God has called them to be! I also learned in this season how to follow the leading of the Holy Spirit on a whole new level. I threw out some of the more structured 'studies' I had used in the past, and just opened the word of God… and we read. And we listened for His voice. And we felt His presence with us. We would put on a worship song and just soak in His presence, just learning how to **BE WITH JESUS**, with no agenda but to be His children and enjoy Him. We learned that during these times, He would speak or touch us or remind us of a scripture or song… and we would share it with the group and follow His lead. This has become my new norm, my favorite way to mentor, and the way I wish I had led groups my whole thirty years prior… but God uses it all. And I decided to just enjoy the gift of this season!

Apprentice. In the introduction to this book, I began by setting this foundation: *More is caught than taught.* Apprentices are trained on the job, trying and failing, and learning as they go! I began to take Bailey and Jasmine with me when I was asked to speak at different churches or Women's Conferences, and often I would ask them to share a short testimony. They were nervous at first, but quickly saw how God would help them be themselves, share their stories, and be a blessing to the people in the room. I would ask them to be part of the ministry team, pray for people, or share any prophetic word that God might be giving them. They were stepping into ministry before they knew what was happening. And they were made for it!

Jasmine stepped out in faith and applied for a Regional Director position with DELIGHT Ministries, (a college ministry for women), where she had first felt the healing joy and love of Jesus! Guess what the job description was? She was to MENTOR over 120 young college leaders who were, in turn, in charge of their campus' chapter of Delight. She was to help train them, stay in touch with them weekly, go visit their chapter meetings and take the leaders out for coffee dates. She traveled all over the Midwest, on frosty mornings and icy roads, and entrusted herself to the Father who promised to be with the girl who 'didn't like to drive!' She oversaw more than 24 chapters/and visited as many college campuses; often sharing her own personal testimony and becoming a beloved mentor to so many who looked up to her.

And the Ripples of Heaven continue. One life, changed by Jesus, can change the lives of 120+ women who are leading chapters of 30,

50, or 70 or more women each, who change entire college campuses for Jesus, who enter into Godly marriages that produce Godly children who grow up learning about the Jesus who loves them...

And the ripples become waves and waves of love that can truly change the whole world.

(**Final Note**: Our youngest son married this precious girl, who is now both my daughter in spirit – and in law. How good is our God?)

Jasmine's Story in Her Words

No matter what mess I've been in or what new season of life I was entering, I've been able to learn and hear the Lord's heart through my mentors. I have gained more wisdom sitting with them for one hour than I had previously by sitting in church services for years. It created a yearning for more of the Lord – through every verse of scripture read and every discussion had. It's deeper than having a counselor who just listens; it's having a real life person who wants to speak truth and clarity from the Lord and walk with you through the thick and thin.

God doesn't want us to do life alone; he calls us to be in relationship with others, where I've learned that God has SO MUCH MORE for us than we could ever imagine! From those times together, I've learned HOW to spend my quiet time when I'm alone with the Lord; and how he loves that time with us even more than we do!

Being mentored and being a mentor both require space to be vulnerable, raw, and REAL. It also requires time management and discipline. You can't just show up – you have to be present! I had to learn to ask questions and really listen!

As I became a mentor to others, there were so many times when I said, "Someone once told me..." or "I heard from ...." It's so FUN sharing wisdom I received and passing it on to others. I've had the pleasure to mentor MANY women in a matter of a few months, and there were definitely some HARD conversations! For example, the 'sex talk' is always challenging! Or, as women, the struggle with comparison and striving. Luckily, I was taught by my mentor that it's OK not to have all the answers; I can point them to the Bible and our Father, who is always so happy that we ask!"

GOING DEEPER

I've learned over the last 30 years that inviting others into our lives is more instructional than the best teaching. More IS caught than taught. I decided years ago that whenever I attend any conference, or volunteer in any ministry, or serve, or take a class ... I invite someone to join me. Whenever I am asked to speak at a church or a womens' conference, I always invite a group of 'my girls' to go with me, sometimes to serve or lead worship or give their testimony. This is not only more effective in training, it's TONS more FUN!

Most recently, when asked to mentor three young married women, each of whom have strong leadership gifts, I decided to invite one of my friends from the Moms Mentoring Group to join me in LEADING the group. Now, these younger brides have not just one older woman's perspective, but two! This same friend helped me just this past fall lead a Young Married Women's gathering on the topic of a healthy sex-life within marriage. Finding others I can invite to co-lead not only helps them grow, it brings wisdom, experience, and perspectives to ME – that I had not had before! It keeps getting more fun!

➤ What about you? What are you currently attending, serving in, or volunteering for that you could invite someone to join you? Who might benefit from it and enjoy being WITH you at the same time?

_____

_____

_____

_____

➢ Is there a class you've been wanting to take or a conference you've wanted to attend, or maybe a group you've wanted to start... but felt hesitant? Ask God if there's someone you could invite to do it WITH you? WITH is always more fun!

_____

_____

_____

➢ Is there a leader that you admire that you would love to learn more from? Offer to serve them in some way, help with an event, or volunteer for some of the jobs no one else enjoys! Learning to humbly serve others is to be like Jesus (and Joshua and Samuel and Barnabas and ...). You will learn much and be blessed! Is God bringing someone to mind?

_____

_____

_____

➢ Have you been invited to be part of something in the past that you turned down? It's never too late to contact that person and tell them you'd be interested if other opportunities arise! Remember, learning to initiate and seek out good counsel and experience is the sign of a hungry disciple that Jesus longs to fill with the Bread of Life!

_____

_____

_____

CHAPTER 14

MULTIPLICATION OF JOY
Nancy's Story

"I wanted to freely give away what I've been given, and that has looked like being willing to let a few people that I mentor into my life in an up-close and personal way: letting them see my marriage, how I make decisions, what I love, sharing dance parties with them, making them meals, and fighting for them in prayer!" - Nancy

"But what was sown on good, rich soil represents the one who hears and fully embraces the message of the kingdom. Their lives bear good fruit – some yield a harvest of thirty, sixty, even one hundred times as much as was sown." Matthew 13:23

Good soil. That's a great description of this girl. Nancy not only invites counsel and mentoring into her life, she cultivates the soil of her own heart with the Holy Spirit to be able and ready to receive ALL that He wants to deposit in her from those around her.

Questions. Questions are one of the marks of this girl. She is ALWAYS asking questions; and not just random ones, but ones that invite the teacher to really stop and think, to answer from that deep place of truth, to sow a seed or word worthy of the depth of the question asked.

Nancy comes with questions ready.

Honor. Nancy truly honors everyone around her. She sees with the eyes of her Father the good, the gold, the treasure in people, and she loves to dig and search and glean from the richness in each one. Therefore, people around her rise up to the level with which she sees them, for they want to be as honorable as she makes them feel.

Sowing Seeds. This is what I feel God has called me to do in life: sow the seed of His word and good news through mentoring, teaching, and preaching His word. Ask a farmer where he loves sowing most? The most fertile, good, and rich soils, of course!

Spiritual Daughter. This is what Nanc has become to me!

Mentoring Nancy has truly been one of the greatest joys in my life, 'cause she's just a joy to mentor! If I had a dollar for every hour we have spent together over the past 17 years, I guess I'd be a billionaire by now! Instead, I see a harvest of good fruit that God has produced through years of doing life the Kingdom Way: preparing soil, sowing the seed, cultivating, weeding, protecting, watering, tending, maintaining a consistent climate of God's presence, and eventually reaping a harvest of not only beautiful fruit, but more seeds that are to be sown.

Multiplication. Like ripples that begin from one single pebble. Like a tree that grows from a tiny mustard seed. God loves to take the offering we give Him, and multiply it like crazy. When we become like the little boy who gives his whole lunch – he really gives his ALL – God can multiply our two loaves and five fish to feed the multitudes. This is not just a bible story. This is real. I'm watching it happen in real time. What you sow matters. Your life matters. Every one does.

One life can change the world.

The story? Nancy was one of the sweet Trio that stole my heart when they were in seventh grade! We started studying the bible together. We worked through the emotional junior high years! And they served with me in our Family Ministry called KidStuff, in which they helped me lead the younger kids in choreographed worship of Jesus. We had fun. So much fun, that other junior high kids wanted to be part of our Worship/ Dance team, so we grew from three to 23 within a few months! We rehearsed every Thursday night and led the family service every Sunday morning for over three years. Serving together makes you family!

During these years, we learned that consistency is so key to relationship. The trio and I tried to meet every week, all through high school, and commit to being in this thing for the long haul. Nancy's example of loyalty and commitment led the way for us.

When the trio graduated from high school, Nancy was the only one who went to college close enough that I could travel to easily; so once a week I would drive 30 minutes north to take her out to lunch and hear how college life was going with Jesus! Sometimes we would call the other two to have a four-way call. Sometimes we would drive to Bloomington to see Sarah, or even Tennessee to hug Erin. But always, we spent time in His word, worshiping as we went, and encouraging one another in His ways. I felt a grace to model faithfulness and consistency during a time of many unknowns and changes that college-age kids face. But let's be honest, the good soil of Nancy's heart caused her to be diligent to keep inviting me into her life, even as she was growing up, and busy, and well, you know, a COLLEGE girl!!

Deep relationships take time. For seeds to grow into healthy plants or trees, it takes years to grow down roots that are deep and strong. The trees that end up producing the most fruit are not the ones that transplant every year or two, but rather the ones who can withstand the winds of change and the storms of life and remain rooted! These are the ones that end up producing a crop 60 or 100 times what was sown!

Today's culture is so transient. Families move, dads change jobs; we don't go to school with the same kids from K-12 like our parents did. Our 'social' time is mostly social MEDIA. Our marriages have split, friendships are hard, and we no longer see or remember the value of working through the conflicts, so we just move on. Many of our hearts have been broken and wounded as our roots are pulled up again and again.

This is where you and I can make a difference! Mentoring can be one place in one other person's life (or two) where they can experience the faithfulness that comes from God. The "I'm sticking with you" kind of love that is not dependent on their mood or behavior or performance. The "You are worth it" kind of friendship that says I'll drive to where you are; I'll be there for you; you can count on me. These are the kinds of seeds that grow into fruitful adults, that multiply into healthy relationships, that want the longevity of a healthy marriage and family…

"I don't know what to do," she told me on the phone. "He's currently dating someone from back home. But we have so much fun together. I've never met a guy like this…." And so we began to mentor into the dating season. (more on this story in Nancy's own words below)

"Miss Lori, this is Logan. You and Steve have been like spiritual parents to Nancy. I've talked to her parents. I'm ready to propose. I'd love to sit down and talk with you two about it, and maybe get your help with the surprise proposal plans….."

And we laughed, and we cried, and we rejoiced that the multiplication was happening, and the 'family' was growing, and it was good.

Steve and I were so privileged to not only be part of the proposal surprise and the Engagement party, we were delighted that they asked us to do their premarital mentoring. Again, we were so struck by the humility of Nancy and Logan to ASK for counsel, to seek out wisdom to prepare them for marriage, to humble themselves enough to say THIS is more important than the WEDDING plans… these are the seeds we need to sow for the MARRIAGE… the long term relationship… the planting of a new family that will grow roots down deep in the soil of God's love; that will live out the "I choose you – forsaking all others,

in sickness and health, in plenty and in want ... till death do we part."
Faithfulness. Commitment. Covenant. These are the Kingdom ways of
Jesus lived out and bearing fruit in every-day relationships.

Nancy went on to become the Worship Pastor at our church.
Meaning, she was MY worship pastor, and I played keys under HER
leadership! She and Logan lead an amazing small group of young adults
at our church, that grew so big it had to split and multiply into multiple
small groups. As I continue to host small groups or marriage groups or
even larger women's events, Nancy faithfully comes whenever she can to
help me lead worship or plan or be part of the planting of more seeds.

Nancy has gone on to invite others into mentoring relationships.
These young women whom she pours into learn about loving Jesus,
cultivating their own hearts with Holy Spirit, and becoming good soil
where the seed of God's word can grow. They learn how to hear His voice
and be led by His Spirit as Nancy beautifully models. *And now, these
young women are beginning to turn and mentor others.*

Like ripples from heaven, the love and message of Jesus continues
to change one good-soil-heart after another, after another, after another.

Nancy's Story

There are so many wonderful ways that mentoring has made a
difference in my life. One that comes to mind was my dating season with
Logan – I remember sitting in Ruby Tuesdays and you so graciously and
kindly suggested, "I think there are some blind spots you are missing,
and taking a step back would be healthy and good." Days later when
Logan and I decided to 'take a break' in our relationship, I came over
to your house and cried in your bathroom while you packed for a trip.
Such a significant moment to me because not only were you a voice
of accountability and correction, but a safe place to process and keep
maturing through those decisions. I distinctly remember the week of our

wedding; the Father reminded me that I could feel even more confident in my choice to marry Logan because I was in the safety of discipleship, and you had been honest with me about areas of strengths and weaknesses we needed to work through first.... I was full of gratitude that God uses mentorship to HELP me make really confident and healthy decisions.

Mentoring requires transparency, honesty, and vulnerability. In our years together I feel like I receive so much when I give so much and stay open. Practically, it requires time, and fighting to make it a priority, especially when meeting with all four of us. It also requires forgiveness and humility to stay soft and not take offense.

Mentoring has been such an integral part of my life for so many years now that it honestly feels like joyful overflow to give it away. The story that comes to mind is sitting across the table from a girl I mentored as she walked through a difficult relationship. Tears were streaming down her face and I found myself saying such similar things that you had said to me years before. "I think these are some blind spots, and maybe taking a step back would be healthy; and you are brave enough to do it!" Watching and walking with her through that decision so reminded me of how you did that with me, and I believe it was unto the better for her! (And she agreed in the end!).

Going Deeper

1. In your own words, why do trees with deep roots produce more fruit/why can relationships that stick together through thick and thin produce more fruit and joy?

    _____

    _____

2. How does a farmer 'prepare the soil' and 'tend the soil'? What does he do/add/remove.... Watch for?

    _____

    _____

3. Ask Holy Spirit what steps you could take to prepare or tend to the soil of your heart so that the seeds He has planted can be most fruitful? What to do/add/remove....

_____

_____

_____

_____

_____

_____

4. Have you ever been given counsel from someone you respect that was exactly what you needed at the time, though hard to hear? Share: _____

_____

_____

5. Have you ever been given counsel from someone you respect that you chose to ignore? What happened?

_____

_____

6. Is there a faithful friend, mentor, or mentee that has been in your life a long time, and you realize you have taken them a bit for granted? Take a minute and thank God for them, and then pick up the phone and let them know! Deep roots are beautiful and bring such special joy!

_____

_____

CHAPTER 15

MARRIAGE MENTORING

Connor & Julia's Story

"The love and wisdom we have found in our mentors' example helped us make a beautiful transition from dating into marriage. We are confident that what we have learned from them will continue to have lasting impact on our marriage and our future generations for years to come!" -Stephen & Becca

"Our mentors glow with love for God and each other! Their passion for strong marriages to change culture and families from the inside out is contagious. Listening to their wisdom and watching their faithfulness inspires us to ask better questions, love sacrificially, and keep investing in each other. Learning from them gave us a stocked relational 'tool belt' to help prepare us for whatever comes."
– Luke & Sarah

Steve and I had been married 6-7 years when the pastor at our church invited us to join a Marriage Small Group with the goal of not only strengthening our own marriages, but also to BECOME marriage mentors within our church. We were blessed to have an older couple lead this group who were actual counselors at a nearby university. But this wasn't a college course where we had to learn psychology or get a certification… we were just members of a church who got to learn from an older couple who took us through a simple book on marriage, and modeled for us how to lead others through the same.

Steve and I were both blessed by the grace of God with parents who had healthy marriages. Growing up, we thought this was normal – like every family was like ours were. But as we got older we realized that what we'd been given was, in fact, NOT normal in today's culture; we realized we'd been given a rare gift. Our parents didn't model PERFECT marriages, but they modeled HEALTHY and joyful marriages, causing us to want the same someday. Their modeling was the best kind of MENTORING that there is.

We knew they sometimes had conflicts, but we also got to watch how they apologized and forgave each other and stayed committed to each other through it all. We watched how they HONORED each other and served each other both in public and behind the closed doors of our home. We observed and became part of a family that not only went to church together, but actually lived out their love for Jesus in the every-day happenings of life. We were taught and mentored in the truth of God's word, and today we more readily believe in the faithfulness of God because we saw faithfulness is possible in our parents.

And so we began. As with any first-time mentoring, when we sat across from our first couple, Chris & Loretta, we realized we had no idea what we were doing! LOL! We had the book we were to follow. This part felt easy for me, the teacher; I can facilitate questions. I remember wondering how we were going to do this TOGETHER, though, since I (the teacher) had read tons of books and listened to many teachings… Was my husband 'prepared'?

I'll never forget that first night. I was moving us along, following the book, asking the questions…. Wait. What did Steve just say? Wow. Yes, that's good wisdom. I kept going… Pause. What did he just ask?

That's a really good question; it's not in the book, but … Good heavens; I can't believe he just said that! Look at that: he could really tell what they were really thinking; he went past the 'right answer' and probed deeper. They just came alive; this just got real; and now I was listening. Forget the book.…

And that night I found out my husband has a gift of wisdom and counsel that I had not seen before. Putting ourselves 'out there' actually brought things out of us that we didn't know God had put in! I had thought of him as Steve, the businessman and leader, but now I could see that the son of a Pastor and a Guidance Counselor had actually become a beautiful blend of the two, and could sense what Holy Spirit was saying and revealing in the moment! I'm so thankful that Lori, the talker, was quiet long enough to listen!!

Marriage Mentoring has not only been FUN for Steve and me these past 25+ years, it has been the best thing for OUR marriage! As Steve says, "It keeps us real." We cannot encourage couples with advice that we ourselves are not following! We can't honestly share with them wisdom that we have gleaned over the years if we are not walking in that wisdom ourselves! This is the beautiful thing about ANY kind of mentoring… it keeps you honest! It sharpens you like iron sharpens iron. It calls you higher to live out the things you long to see others live out as well!! Mentoring causes you to REMEMBER what's most important and reminds you of the BASICS, which keeps your own foundation strong and fresh.

We also realized we are thankful for a church that values Marriage MENTORING Relationships (pairing up an older couple with one getting married), as opposed to just attending a class so they can check off a box on the Wedding To-Do List! This allows us to walk through some life together and really get to know them over many months. We can observe how they communicate, how they handle conflict, and what comes up after going to her parents' house! This is much different than just asking a couple getting married to 'attend this Premarital Class', or meet once with the Pastor, so they can move on to the tux shop!

We are honest with them from meeting one: *"This which you are entering into is serious business! It is one of the most sacred and AMAZING gifts that God gives to His children, but it is not easy! It is full of joy unspeakable, but it will also be hard! It is the most rewarding relationship this side of heaven, but it will take work. And intentionality. It requires a choice to invest in this relationship from now till death do you part. Are you willing? Will you commit to meeting consistently with us for at least 10, maybe 12 sessions over these next 6-9 months? Will you commit to doing this God's way and abstaining from sex until after you are joined as one by God? Ie. The Wedding?"* (Yes, we ask this question. We explain that God is the creator of the sexual union. It is His great wedding gift. Sex is to bind a man and a women together in the covenant of marriage like glue bonds together PERMANENTLY. And even if they have engaged in sex before meeting with us, we gladly go over God's wonderful plan and PURPOSE for sex, and ask them to refrain *starting NOW*. This is a wonderful time to mentor them in obedience to Jesus, sacrificing our wills for His, and trusting in His goodness that ALWAYS comes to those who trust and obey. His plan is always for our best, and He is a good Father that can be trusted!)

Steve loves using these months of meeting with couples to call the man into leading and initiating; he models Servant Leadership like Jesus leads His bride, laying down his life, his preferences, and his selfishness for his wife.

I try to use this time to model how to respect my husband, support him well, and be his biggest fan. The wife, too, lays down her life for her man. I also can share my own experiences of Steve supporting me whether I remained at my teaching job, or whether I chose to stay home with our kids. We simply share our story; it's not a perfect one; but it can be used to say, 'This is how we got to this decision – we work together and listen and honor one another. We don't always get it right, in fact here are ways we've really messed it up; but we have learned how to forgive and ask for forgiveness.. '

We've learned that the Gospel message of the grace of Jesus applies in our marriage as much as anywhere in the world. In fact, without Jesus, we really don't know how people make it. He keeps us loving when we don't feel like it, and forgiving even when the other doesn't deserve it. In this world of quid-pro-quo, the unmerited grace of Jesus runs counter-cultural to the world and relationships around us. But oh, how brightly the marriage shines when the world sees the Gospel played out in that marriage, and their friends run to them and ask, 'How do you love each other like that?'

These young couples have become so dear to us. Many have grown up and we proudly now call friends. But always, we will stay available to them. We try to check in on them, and see how their marriage is doing! We meet up when we can, and we remind them to ask for help when they need it! The beautiful thing about Marriage Mentoring is that we aren't just in relationship until the WEDDING; we remain available and in their lives long into the MARRIAGE! Cause let's be honest, getting to the altar is only the beginning!

GENERATIONAL IMPACT

We think it no coincidence that one of the first consequences of sin entering the world in the Garden of Eden was to cause the woman to accuse the man and the man to accuse the woman. Mutual respect and selfless love went out the window. Made in the likeness and image of God, this was when we INSTEAD started acting more like the enemy, whose very name is Accuser.

And that old Accuser is still intent on destroying marriages today. You don't need this book to inform you of the incredible statistics on divorce, broken families, kids who grow up without a dad, etc etc.

God intended Marriage to be the foundation of His Kingdom family, from which healthy kids are raised, strong communities are formed, and culture thrives… when we have Kingdom marriages.

Therefore, Steve and I look at Marriage Mentoring as more than just a 'way to serve'; we see it as one small counter- measure we can take against the breakdown of our very society. Jesus is always the answer, and His Kingdom ways are always the RIGHT ways; but we are amazed at the numbers of young people who have not been exposed to His ways, nor mentored in how they actually apply to every day life and love and marriage. *In today's world, we need Mentors who know Jesus to invest in the up & coming next generation!*

Wouldn't it be marvelous if we could say that our small pebble thrown into the lake of building strong marriages caused ripples from heaven to change an entire family line, or community, or even nation?

Steve and I are blessed that over 35 couples have allowed us to walk through the ups and downs of their life journeys with them. We thank God for their commitments to keep their marriage a priority and to remain aware of the holy weightiness of fighting for strong marriages in today's world. We hope this might be stirring something in some of you married couples… this is serious business! *You are needed. And you can do this!*

Conner & Julia

This couple's story is special to us for many reasons, but the thing that makes their story different is that they approached us and asked us to mentor them BEFORE THEY WERE ENGAGED!

Conner & Julia had been dating for nearly two years. They had reached that point in a relationship where they knew they either needed to move intentionally towards marriage, or decide to part ways. Should he finish school in this town? Should she take the job in that city? How serious IS this relationship? And, are our 'differences' the kind that make us complement each other? Or are we SO different that we would be wise to move on?

We have the greatest respect for Conner and Julia! In fact, we are now on a campaign to start a whole NEW kind of mentoring: **PRE-ENGAGEMENT MENTORING!** Think about it. This is brilliant! Most couples come to us long after they've made up their minds: By the time she says YES, the venue is booked, and the dress is bought… the train has left the station. In other words, if red flags come up in premarital mentoring, or we find we have some serious concerns and suggest they take time to work through some brokenness or get counseling … few couple we know of are willing to stop and work on their issues at this point. BUT - by asking for counsel/mentoring BEFORE a ring is bought, they can honestly and humbly talk about their relationship, and be courageous enough to truly want to know: What do you think? Are there any red flags we don't see?

This is the way Conner & Julia approached us. I honestly think the smartest people I know are the ones who know to ask for help. Who are humble enough to say, "This is new for us. We are young and in love. We want your input, we are seeking your wise counsel. What do you think?" It was such a great joy to sit down with them WHILE DATING and talk about how they communicate, what their future goals were, how compatible were their interests, and more importantly, their faith journeys? Were they on the same page with God? Would they agree on how to worship and serve Him, and how to raise the kids?

We are praying their example catches the attention of others… and spreads like Ripples from Heaven! We worked through many sessions with them, talked through some rough patches, and got to rejoice with tears in our eyes when he got down on one knee and she said a *confident YES!*

This did not guarantee a perfect marriage for these two, but it did equip them with tools to make a wise decision on WHOM to marry; and we enjoyed every minute of the next months of pre*marital* mentoring, giving them more tools to work with for the seasons that were to come. As I type this, we are still in close relationship with Conner & Julia. You should know they have had their ups and downs, the greatest of joys, and some really hard days, too. But the difference was, they had a foundation in the word of God. They had some tools in their belts to get out when they needed to work on their stuff. And they have at least one older couple who adores them and has been there when they humbled themselves, picked up the phone, and met us for coffee to talk.

To us, this is a beautiful picture of the Kingdom of God at work. This is one of our favorite examples of the brilliant example of Mentoring that Jesus gave us. We are to BE THERE for each other, to encourage, strengthen, support, speak truth, and love deeply. (See the entire New Testament for more examples of this....)

And AS DISCIPLES, we also are called to HUMBLE ourselves under God's mighty hand, to seek Godly counsel, to ask for help when we need it, to knock and keep on knocking. To allow others to know us authentically and speak into our lives and trust that our good Father speaks to us through the lips of those He has surrounded us with. To admit that we don't know it all, we fail often, and allow OTHERS to know that as well: that's the Kingdom life.

"This is the message we heard from Jesus and now declare to you: God is light, and there is no darkness in him at all. So we are lying if we say we have fellowship with God but go on living in spiritual darkness; we are not practicing the truth. But, if we are living in the light, as God is in the light, then we have fellowship with each other, and the blood of Jesus, his Son, cleanses us from all sin." 1 John 1: 5-7

GOING DEEPER

1. Are you in that 'dating' season of life? Is there an older couple whose marriage you admire or respect, whom you could just ask if you could sit down at a coffee shop and ask them some questions about their relationship? And possibly invite them to speak into yours? Start with just one meeting; see how it goes!

   _____

   _____

2. Are you married? How long has it been since you 'invested' in your marriage: gone to a marriage conference or retreat, joined a marriage group or class, read a good book on marriage together? Or just reached out to another couple and asked for some 'help' or mentoring advice? There are always other couples who are a few years down the road with a wealth of experience to share! Ask Holy Spirit what next steps you two could take to invest and grow together? These investments ALWAYS have great returns!

   _____

   _____

   _____

3. As you read this chapter, did you find yourself wishing you had had a bit more wisdom or counsel from others before YOU got married? Are there specific things that could have really helped you if you had only known "that?" Do you feel the nudge from Holy Spirit: could it be He's just asking you to share YOUR story? Simply share what God has taught you? Ask Him: Is there a young couple in your sphere of influence who is in the 'dating' scene? One you could invite out for ice cream and just get to know them? (hint: EVERY couple loves to tell their story when asked: 'How did you meet? How long have you been dating? What's your favorite

thing about this person?"

_____

_____

_____

_____

4. What next steps might God be leading you to take? (Reminder, give your spouse some time to think about this, maybe to read this chapter on mentoring! Being on the same page is sort of critical to the mission!!)

_____

_____

_____

This is really that simple. Marriage mentoring is just sharing your lives and your story with a couple a few years behind you in the journey! And the Heavenly Ripple effect means that BOTH couples end up being blessed as you spend time encouraging and learning and becoming more like Jesus in your marriages!

(For more insights on Marriage, see our book: **Marriage Moments,** wherever books are sold; or go to **marriagemomentsimpact.com**)

CHAPTER 16

PARENTS & GRANDPARENTS

24/7 Mentors

"Train up a child in the way he should go; even when he is old he will not depart from it." Proverbs 22:6

Our oldest son, Clay, was leading worship at the church where he is on staff. We went to worship with their congregation, amazed every time that "that's our little Clay-man!" (Of course, we don't SAY that out loud since he's a pastor and all....)

He was in the middle of leading a beautiful worship song, the instrumental bridge was playing, and he just began to speak, "Who may ascend the hill of the Lord? Who may stand in His holy place? He who has clean hands and a pure heart, who does not lift up his soul to an idol or swear by what is false...." And my heart caught in my throat, and the tears came streaming down my face; because instead of seeing grown-man Clay, I suddenly could only see six-year-old Clay standing next to his four-year old little brother John, and they were reciting that Psalm 24 to their dad as part of our homeschool memorization. And instead of hearing Clay's 28-year-old voice, I only heard his six-year-old voice, joining with his brother's as they shouted and stumbled, "... he who has CLEAN HANDS and a PURE HEA.... STOP IT, JOHN!" "No, you sop it Cayman…." As he pushed his brother away from him. And my voice, "Ok, guys, don't push. Let's try again…"

And as Clay recited the Psalm, from somewhere deep in his memory, somewhere deep in his heart, my own heart became a puddle on the floor; a puddle of gratitude and awe and wonder at a God who could possibly be so faithful that seeds we plant when they are young really DO grow and sprout and produce a harvest of fruit when they are older. The emotions just waved over me, and I fell to my knees and knew that only a good, good Father like ours could ever work such wonders and allow us to partner in it with Him to shape a life, a little heart, to love their Abba God.

If you are a parent, you are a mentor. If you are a Grandparent, you KNOW you are a mentor! And if you are a Parent or Grandparent, you are THEE MOST IMPORTANT MENTORS your children will ever have.

Of all the mentoring I have ever done, being a Mom has been my favorite. Of all the privileges I have been given, being Steve's wife and Clay & John's mom has been my highest. Of all the gifts I am so grateful for, getting to mother, love, train, model, teach, raise, and enjoy our two boys has been my deepest and most profound joy.

"Listen, O Israel! The Lord our God is one. You shall love the Lord your God with all your heart and with all your soul and with all your might. And these words that I command you today shall be on your heart. You shall teach them diligently to your children and shall talk of them when you sit in your house, and when you walk by the way, and when you lie down, and when you rise. You shall bind them as a sign on your hand, and they shall be as frontlets between your eyes. You shall write them on the doorposts of your house and on your gates." Deuteronomy 6: 4-6 ESV

You, oh Parent or Grandparent, Aunt or Uncle, YOU have the most remarkable opportunity. You get to introduce your babies and toddlers to the world, and to the God that made the world, and to the place that they have within it. You literally get to shape their world view. You get to be the one who shows them the bird's nest and tells them that God made the bird who made the nest, and God made the song that the bird is now singing! You get to be the one to say, "LOOK! LOOK what God made for us to enjoy! Look and see the miracle of the flower opening up, or the corn as it grows so tall! Isn't God amazing!? Look at the cows that know how to eat the grass, and the eagles who can soar through the sky! Isn't our Father good?"

From day one, you get to be the one that shows them that God is not someone we go to visit on Sunday mornings alone, but that He is the one we talk to throughout every day, the one we worship and thank for every good thing, and the One who loves them and knows them and is ALWAYS with them, so they know they are never alone.

And like the passage above, YOU get to be the one who determines what they think about, what they are surrounded by, and what is most important in life! TRULY, more is CAUGHT THAN TAUGHT, so THEE MOST IMPORTANT THING you could do to mentor your children and disciple them IS TO LOVE THE LORD **YOUR** GOD! It's to BE a disciple YOURSELF! It's to study His word and listen for His voice for you! It's to choose to Worship God and model that this is most important for your OWN life, it is your daily joy, and not just something we do on Sundays! And even when you discipline, remember that THAT is actually DISCIPLING, as the purpose of it all is to train them to obey Jesus, because He loves us so and His ways can be trusted!

More will be caught than taught, so HOW you speak to them matters. How you ask for forgiveness matters, and how readily you repent and remind them how much YOU need Jesus to save YOU matters…. More will be caught than taught! They will hear what you say, but more than that, they will SEE how you prioritize your life and your time… and what really matters. More will be caught than taught! May you passionately pursue the Jesus whom you so passionately want them to follow. May you Love Him with all of YOUR heart, so they will want to do the same.

LOVE THE LORD YOUR GOD! Write it on their nursery walls! And live it out in every kiss you give them! Talk about it when you greet the new day, and thank Him when you get to eat good food! Turn on the worship music instead of the TV, and live in the cultivated presence of God as you sing to Him together throughout your days! Make up your own songs, and dance together as you celebrate Who our God is and how much He loves us!

And oh, teach them His ways, His Word, His instructions of love to us His children! Saturate them with the Word of God: write it on the doorposts of your home; talk about it when you are going to bed and read it when you rise each day. Memorize it and recite it as you walk or drive along the road; write it, study it, and teach them to hear God speaking directly to them through it!

Someday, twenty years later, you may hear it come back through their mouths and out of their hearts to be a blessing to others. And you will weep for joy.

"O my people listen to my instructions. Open your ears to what I am saying, for I will speak to you in a parable. I will teach you hidden lessons from our past – stories we have heard and known, stories our ancestors handed down to us. We will not hide these truths from our children; we will tell the next generation about the glorious deeds of the Lord, about his power and his mighty wonders!

For he issued his laws to Jacob; he gave his instructions to Israel. He commanded our ancestors to teach them to their children, so the next generation might know them - even the children not yet born - and they in turn will teach their own children. So, each generation should set its hope anew on God, not forgetting his glorious miracles and obeying his commands." Ps. 78: 1-7

This past year, Steve and I became Grandparents. And yes, our hearts have been stolen by little Millie Kate! When a brand-new generation begins, it causes you to want to know about the many generations that have gone before. You suddenly become aware that you are a link in a much bigger chain, and that many of the good things in our lives are because someone many generations ago paid a price for or prayed for your mom or your dad and possibly prayed for you!

And while we want to teach and train from God's word, let us not miss the message of Psalm 78: we are to tell them our STORIES! Our true TESTIMONIES OF ALL GOD HAS DONE IN OUR LIVES! Not just history lessons from the pages of scripture, but real-life encounters and miracles that GOD HAS DONE FOR US!

We want Millie Kate to know that her Great Granddad Don Orander was the kindest Pastor who loved people so well. We will tell her the stories of his compassionate decision to fight racial injustice in the 1960's by painting his face black and living on the streets of Chicago so that he could understand what his black brothers were going through. We will tell her how he was at Salem when Martin Luther King marched with many across the bridge, and her Great Granddad was there to help others sign up for the right to vote.

I will share with Millie how her Great-Great Grandfather Bob Childs spent two years risking his life and fighting for our freedoms in WWII, and wrote letters back home to HIS two little boys and wife, my Grandmother, whom he missed with all his heart.

I will tell Millie that when I was just a bit older than she, I would sit on the front row of my Grandparents' church where my Granddaddy John directed the choir, and my Grandmother Lavonne played the organ for over 30 years. And how one day as I sat there, I just looked at the cross and listened to my mom (Millie's Great Grandmother Nancy) singing. I remember looking over at my Granddad and wondering why his eyes were closed. But then I realized he wasn't sleeping, he was worshiping his Jesus whom my momma was singing about:

"I'd rather have Jesus than silver or gold. I'd rather be His than have riches untold. I'd rather have Jesus than anything this world affords today...." And I saw the tears streaming down my mother's face, and I remember thinking, "She is not singing to us. She doesn't even know we're here. She's singing to her Jesus. Wow. I want to know Him like that. God, I want to love you like that...."

And so began my own journey, because my parents and my grandparents were living their own lives and loving their own Jesus, and I caught their faith and began to love their Jesus ... and He became my very own.

I will tell her how her Great-Great-Great Grandmother Blanche, whom we called Gram, loved Jesus, too. And how the last time I visited her, when she didn't even know who we were or recognize her family, I thought it was sad... Until. Until we heard her singing, "And He walks with me, and He talks with me, and He tells me I am His own...." And we knew that even though her body was wasting away, yet her spirit was being renewed day by day and still loving her Jesus.

I will tell her the story of how her Great-Great Granddaddy John received a miracle of healing when stomach pains had become too much to bear. And the time that her Uncle John's knee was healed through prayer. We will tell her of how her Aunt Jasmine received a prophetic word in a crowd of over 500 people, and how God spoke to her and Uncle John through the prophet who came to town. We will take time to tell her the story of when her Pappi (Steve) started his own business, and we stepped out in faith and trusted in God and sank all our life's savings into a small business.... And how God miraculously brought people who asked to work for her Pappi, for free, until he could pay them… and how God did miracle after miracle to grow a small, no-name business from 3 people to 30, then to 60, and just 7 years later, to 120… and how we would go and pray over the office, and anoint each doorway with oil, and ask for God's favor and pray for His blessing over all who worked there……

Yes. We will tell the next generations the great stories of our God. Of how REAL He is, and how powerfully He's worked in our lives. We will NOT FORGET the goodness and love of our God and the many ways He has blessed us. We will cultivate grateful hearts and minds that live in wonder and can say with confidence, "How GREAT is OUR God!"

Tell your Stories. Pass them on to the next generation. It is up to us to pass the baton, or the baton will not be passed! The rest of Psalm 78 describes what happens when we do NOT pass on our testimonies. Then we forget. Then the next generation does not know. And they do not worship our God, nor trust in His good ways.

This is our time, people. This is our hour. Tell the next generation the mighty deeds of the Lord IN YOUR LIFE. THIS IS MENTORING. THIS IS DISCIPLING. THIS IS passing it on in the context of the most constant of RELATIONSHIPS… where your kids see you on good days and bad days, when your heart's happy or sad.

May EVERY day be a day of grace. And every conversation be saturated with LOVE, as we abide in the LOVE of our Jesus.

"He commanded our ancestors to teach them to their children, so the next generation might know them – even the children not yet born – and they in turn will teach their own children...." Psalm 78: 7

Like Ripples of heaven from generations past, from the great cloud of witnesses cheering us on, may our stories of God spread and continue and multiply...wave after rippling wave.... until the knowledge of the glory of God covers the face of the earth.

GOING DEEPER

If you are the first generation in your family to be a Christian, and you think you do not have these stories to pass on, hear the good news: YOU ARE STARTING THE WAVE! YOU get to be the first to experience and recount the stories of God in your life, in spite of whatever your pasts may have been! And you can start a whole new generational CHAIN of testimonies of the goodness of your God! Start the wave!

How has God been real in your life? Has he moved in miraculous ways, or blessed you beyond measure? Has he rescued you from 'the lion's mouth' or impossible circumstances? How has He saved you? TELL YOUR STORIES! Write them down!

If you do NOT come from a Christian background, it does not mean that Christ was not in your background! They just may not have known it! There are still crazy GOOD stories of your ancestors that you will want to pass down. And maybe YOU can be the one to point out how God was there all along, for only HE could have done this , or that... or led them here... **TELL YOUR STORIES!**

1. What stories are coming to mind right now?

   _____

   _____

   _____

   _____

   _____

   _____

2. What is your greatest prayer for your kids or grandkids? How can you cultivate that in your OWN life so that you may model the authentic expression of it?

_____

_____

_____

_____

_____

3. What new creative ways are you now pondering in order to teach your kids and grandkids the Word of God? What next steps will you take? How can you develop consistency, which will be the building blocks of a Disciple's disciplines!

_____

_____

_____

_____

_____

4. How can you cultivate an atmosphere of Worship in your home? In the car? As you take walks? Ask God to show you all the opportunities you have to worship WITH your kids in joy and fun... start when they are young! What ideas is Holy Spirit whispering to you?

_____

_____

_____

_____

_____

5. And how can you begin to invite Jesus into every conversation? How can you teach them to listen for His voice, that He is always speaking, and that He loves to answer when we ask Him questions! Practice. Consistently. Ask this one often, then listen, then write: "Father, what do you love about me today?" (And don't forget to do this yourself, with them, and share your answers too!)

_____

_____

_____

_____

_____

_____

_____

_____

_____

_____

_____

_____

_____

_____

_____

_____

_____

_____

____

CHAPTER 17

DISCIPLESHIP IS PASSING ON YOUR FLAME
MENTORING IS COMING
CLOSE ENOUGH THAT
OTHERS CATCH
ON FIRE

"All the believers were meeting together in one place. Suddenly, there was a sound from heaven like the roaring of a mighty wind, and it filled the house where they were sitting. Then what looked like flames or tongues of fire appeared and settled on each of them. And everyone present was filled with the Holy Spirit and began speaking in other languages, as the Holy Spirit gave them this ability. . . All the believers devoted themselves to the apostles' teaching, and to fellowship, and to sharing in meals, and to prayer. A deep sense of awe came over them all and the apostles performed many miraculous signs and wonders. And all the believers met together in one place and shared everything they had. They sold their property and possessions and shared the money with those in need. They worshiped together at the Temple each day, met in homes for the Lord's Supper, and shared their meals with great joy and generosity – all the while praising God and enjoying the goodwill of all the people. And each day the Lord added to their fellowship those who were being saved." Acts 2: 1-4, 42-47

Today, as I type these words, it is March 8, 2021. I believe with all my heart that we are living in the most amazing and exciting time! I believe that God is once again pouring out His Spirit, that a Great Awakening has begun, and that it is going to spread like wildfire, until the whole world is on fire for Jesus!

And when that happens, **we are going to need Fathers and Mothers-in-the-Faith who will welcome home the children to the Family of God and help them grow up into their true selves: now children of God.** We are going to need MENTORS whose hearts are burning for Jesus who will come close enough in relationships that those around them will catch on fire as well.

To disciple is to raise up Burning Ones for Jesus.

To disciple by mentoring is to come close enough to share your flame, causing others to burn with love for Him.

John, the disciple of Jesus, burned with love for his Savior like no other. He walked with Him and learned from Him while He was on the earth. John stood by Jesus' mother and watched Him die on the cross, suffering in our place. Three days later, John was one of the first to run to the empty tomb to find that it was TRUE: Jesus ROSE from the grave and IS ALIVE! And John was there on that day of Pentecost, that we read above, when Jesus poured out the great gift of the Father: the promised Holy Spirit – who would be for John all that Jesus had been and MORE! For now, Jesus was not just WITH them, He was now living IN them by His Spirit.

John lived out the rest of his life sharing this most astounding good news wherever He went! He could not KEEP from telling anyone who would listen about the love of this Jesus and the good news of Life that He offers all people. John went on to plant churches in different areas, spreading the good news across the world like RIPPLES OF HEAVEN; like flames of fire that could not be put out, even by the persecution that came upon the church and those who followed Jesus!

They tried to silence John and Peter by threatening to arrest them if they continued to teach in 'this Jesus' name'. The two responded by saying, *"We cannot stop speaking about all we have seen and heard."* And they did not. They were arrested, persecuted, beaten, and many disciples were killed. They tried to kill John multiple times, but God miraculously kept him alive. So, they exiled him to a deserted island called Patmos to keep him from making more disciples; so that he would stop telling others of the love and forgiveness of Jesus.

But on that island, John received a visitation. Jesus came to him and encountered him there. John received a fresh Revelation of Jesus and continued to enjoy deep and constant fellowship with the One he loved so dearly. He wrote this:

"I, John, am your brother and your partner in suffering and in God's Kingdom and in the patient endurance to which Jesus calls us. I was exiled to the island of Patmos for preaching the word of God and for my testimony about Jesus. It was the Lord's Day, and I was worshiping in the Spirit. Suddenly, I heard behind me a loud voice like a trumpet blast. It said, 'Write in a book everything you see and send it to the seven churches in the cities of ...'

"When I turned to see who was speaking to me, I saw seven gold lampstands. And standing in the middle of the lampstands was someone like the Son of Man. He was wearing a long robe with a gold sash across his chest. His head and his hair were white like wool, as white as snow. And his eyes were like flames of fire...

When I saw him, I fell at his feet as if I were dead. But he laid his right hand on me and said, 'Don't be afraid! I am the First and the Last. I am the living one. I died, but look – I am alive forever and ever! And I hold the keys of death and the grave." Revelation 1: 9-14, 17-18

To disciple, you must first see Jesus and His eyes of fire burning with love for YOU. He still reveals Himself to those who ask and wait on Him! Then, you cannot help but **fix** your eyes on Him until you are transformed by His gaze, immersed in that love that burns away everything and anything that hinders love .... Until all that is left of you and me is Love.

To Disciple is to train others in tending the fire of love for Jesus!

Discipleship has long been equated with training others to worship, read their bibles, obey, pray, surrender our will for His, and be part of a church or community of believers. But none of these is the END GOAL: each of these is so important, but they are USED to help us TEND THE FIRE.

The goal of all of this mentoring and discipling is to love Jesus with all our heart, soul, mind, and strength; and to keep that fire of love glowing and growing and burning bright!

Because here's the secret to it all: If I love Jesus with all that I am, and my heart is burning with love and devotion for Him, then I WILL worship! I WILL read the Bible! I WILL obey what He asks of me! I will pray and listen and spend time in His glorious presence! I WILL gladly surrender my will for His WILL! I WILL! I will do ALL THESE THINGS... BECAUSE I WILL WANT TO! I will do ALL these things because I LOVE HIM and long to know Him more! The more I know of Him, the more I love Him, and the more I love Him, the more I want to know Him! And the ripple effect of Heaven begins in my own heart; the flames of love for Jesus are fanned into greater flames that grow hotter and brighter with every year!

So, the goal of discipleship is to raise up Burning Ones for Jesus.

And the goal of Mentoring is to be so close to others in relationship that they CATCH on fire with love for Jesus because they came close to our flame!

In A Word? Encounter: Mentors lead them Directly to Jesus

The most effective way to Disciple someone is to teach them how to LIVE in the presence of Jesus! The most important thing we mentors can do is pray for and assist them in AWAKENING to His abiding presence within them 24/7/365.

Practically speaking, I now start my Mentoring times with each of these disciples or small groups by WORSHIPING Jesus! Taking time as a small group of two or three or five to WORSHIP Him together. *"Come into His gates with Thanksgiving, and His courts with Praise. Give thanks to Him and praise His name!"* This is how we enter in. Beginning with worship lifts our self-focus to focus on HIM! And when we SEE Him and sing to Him, we are declaring WHO He is and coming into agreement with the Truth that Jesus is King! He is worthy of it all! He alone is the desire of my heart!

Sometimes, I will have our group just be silent before Him, and listen for His voice! Sometimes, we will put on worship music and just SOAK in His presence, training them how to be still and awaken to His presence here with us. Right now. Right here. He is here. (Even as you read these words.)

We often will use a prompt, in which we will ask God a question, and then write or journal His voice: what HE is saying. This trains them that God is always speaking, and He is a good Shepherd who loves it when His sheep stop long enough to hear His voice!

All of these are means of ENCOUNTERING God! Not just reading about Him, but inviting Him to speak as we read His word. Stopping to sense what Holy Spirit is saying right now, through His word or pro-phetic pictures or . . .! He is here!

Not just singing songs about Him, but singing TO Him, because we've been reminded that He is among us. Not just praying the right words, but actually talking to the Living One who loves us and wants to talk back and actually have CONVERSATION with us, even in small groups.

This is training /discipling others to have ENCOUNTERS with Je-sus. This is the joy of Holy Spirit in us: He is constantly revealing Jesus to us, even as John encountered Him on the Isle of Patmos. Holy Spirit is the Spirit of Wisdom and REVELATION ... to all of us , every day, every hour!

To disciple is to awaken others to the presence of Jesus within them by His Holy Spirit. To disciple is to bring our disciples into His presence through worship or the Word or listening prayer ... close enough that they can see His eyes of fire and realize how much He loves them!

Because when we see His blazing eye of fire, burning with love for us, and the smile of joy upon His face, shining brighter than the sun, we will be baptized again with fire, immersed again in waves of life-chang-ing, overwhelming love and grace and forgiveness and acceptance and belonging and devotion and...

And we will be changed! We will become like Him! And that is what discipleship is all about. One life changed and burning with love for Jesus, will draw others to the warmth of their fire, and others will be set on fire, causing revival fire to spread across this earth that needs Him so desperately!

Like Ripples of Heaven, I pray you will both reach out to be men-tored and will eventually choose to mentor others, discipling them through relationship and multiplying the disciples of Jesus like ripples across the water, until earth looks like Heaven, and the Lamb receives the reward for His suffering.

> *"Then the angel showed me a river with the water of life, clear as crystal, flowing from the throne of God and of the Lamb. It flowed (rippled) down the center of the main street. On each side of the river grew a tree of life, bearing twelve crops of fruit, with a fresh crop each month. The leaves were used for medicine to heal the nations." Revelation 22:1-2*

GOING DEEPER

1. As you finish this book, what action steps is Father God asking you take right now? Go. Do it. Obey. And be blessed with great joy! (John 15: 8-17)

_____

_____

_____

_____

_____

_____

_____

_____

_____

_____

_____

_____

_____

"Our Beloved Father, dwelling in the heavenly realms, may the glory of your name be the center on which our lives turn. Manifest your kingdom realm, and cause your every purpose to be fulfilled on earth, just as it is in heaven." Matthew 6: 9-10 TPT